The Friendship Book

of Francis Gay

D. C. THOMSON & CO., LTD.
London Glasgow Manchester Dundee

A Thought
For Each Day
In 1986

The world is a book and every step turns a new page.

LAMARTINE

AT REST

Greenest of trees on the hillside,
  Bluest of waters below,
And fishing boats anchored safely
  Where a gentle tide ebbs slow.
This, their day of rest and peace,
The seventh day, when labours cease.

JANUARY

WEDNESDAY—JANUARY 1.

IN the air-raid on Coventry on the night of 14th November 1940, only 30 out of 1000 buildings in the city centre were undamaged and many were completely destroyed. Of the old cathedral only the outer walls and the spire remained.

But during the rebuilding, the remains of the old cathedral were linked with the new, so that old and new became one entity.

Old and New Year surely is a time for linking together in our thoughts, glad memories of the past and great hopes for the future, to make the present really worth living.

THURSDAY—JANUARY 2.

WHEN the Sherpas of remote Nepal asked Sir Edmund Hillary if he could help them start up a school, he raised the necessary money—some £5000—by giving lectures all round the world. Then he went back to Nepal with the money and materials, a journey which involved a walk of 150 miles after leaving the plane. At the end of this trek he cheerfully joined in the actual building of the school, as did most of the community, including the children. Sir Edmund stayed until the work was finished and he was guest of honour at the opening ceremony.

Since that first school, 22 others have been built in Nepal. " Climbing Everest was only a stepping stone," he said afterwards. " Building the next hospital and a bridge for the Sherpas was more important than the first footprints on top of the world."

WHEN we go to visit our friend Mary we usually look at her calendar. It is one of the " tear-off " kind with a saying for each day of the year. One I remember in particular said, " Happiness is a journey, not a destination."

" A Happy New Year!" we say to people, but happiness is not something we have to reach as a kind of goal; it is something we find as we go on our way through the New Year, giving ourselves with zest to the task in hand, and to service and to helpfulness.

SATURDAY—JANUARY 4.

WHEN the Lady of the House and I visit some of our old cathedrals we like to turn up the seats in the choir stalls and look at the carvings underneath. If you have done this you will know how many of them are of a humorous nature—an animal dancing or a pig playing the pipes, for example. One we saw in Carlisle Cathedral was of a woman holding her husband by the hair and beating him! Many seem to caricature in a humorous way the follies and foibles of the old monks.

At first sight, these may seem rather strange decorations to be found in church, but I think they are reminders that laughter, too, has its place. It sometimes seems to be thought that the more solemn we are, the more religious we are. It isn't true! As the writer of the Book of Proverbs put it, " A merry heart doeth good like a medicine."

SUNDAY—JANUARY 5.

THE Lord is my shepherd; I shall not want.

Psalm 23, 1.

THE FRIENDSHIP BOOK

A little child was asked by a friend of mine the other day how old she was. " Old?" exclaimed the child indignantly. " I'm not old at all, I'm quite new!"

A childlike reaction, perhaps, but there's more than a grain of truth in it, isn't there? Its not how *old* we are that matters—it's how *new* and expectant we are in our outlook on life.

SOMETIMES a task seems insurmountable and we feel it can never be done. It seemed that way to Heather Campbell one morning when she arrived to unlock the gates to the playschool—there, piled high outside the gate, obstructing the pavement, was a great heap of golden sand. It should have been filling the pit in the playground, but obviously the driver, delivering early and finding the gates locked, had dumped it. " And we haven't even a decent spade, let alone a wheelbarrow!" groaned Heather despairingly.

The children fell on the sand joyfully when they arrived. " Come on, let's make sand pies," yelled Colin brandishing his sandbucket. " Not here," said Heather firmly, " you must wait until the sand's been moved into the sandpit." Colin looked at her for a moment, then bending down he scooped up a bucketful of sand, and marched with it to the pit. Within a few moments all the children were doing the same thing.

Bit by bit the " mountain " was moved until it was all in the sandpit. What had seemed impossible was achieved through sheer determination.

" You know," said Heather, " I think the children appreciate the sandpit all the more for having worked so hard to fill it."

WINTER WALKERS

THE FRIENDSHIP BOOK

A CHURCH member wrote in a letter to her parish magazine, " The other day a friend from the church came to see me. I don't usually talk about my troubles, but she sounded so sympathetic and understanding that I did venture to mention something that was greatly worrying me.

" When I had finished, she nodded and said, ' Now, what can we do about that?' It was the word ' we ' which made all the difference to me. I realised how true it is to say, ' A trouble shared is a trouble halved '."

A LADY kneeling behind a young man praying in church was startled to notice that although he was neatly dressed, the soles of his boots had holes in them through which she could see his socks.

Not unusual towards the end of last century when poverty was rife. Yet the lady knew that the young man was Edward Wilson, a medical student at St George's Hospital, Battersea.

Years later she vividly remembered the episode. By then Dr Wilson had become famous as a naturalist, author and above all an explorer. He accompanied Captain Scott on his expeditions and died with him at the South Pole on their last journey. Dr Wilson's physical courage was outstanding, but even more so was his moral courage. Before their deaths Captain Scott penned the tribute: " I hold him mainly responsible for the relationship which has existed among us."

One of Wilson's favourite mottoes was: " Better to say nothing than to condemn; to laugh with rather than criticise, and so be much happier!"

FRIDAY—JANUARY 10.

TODAY I pass on to you these inspiring lines by the Scottish poet, Mary Milne:

Life is a highway broad and smooth,
A narrow rough-track lane,
A pasture green, where joy abounds,
A dark wood filled with pain,
A long, hard hill away ahead
That dragging feet must climb,
Which yet, when conquered, oft reveals
A vale of peace sublime;
A wilderness of waste land,
A garden tilled with care,
A deep ravine of hatred,
A crest of love so fair.
'Tis bones with age protesting,
'Tis healthy, searching youth,
A sea of cruel deception,
A rock of much sought truth.
Life is a mighty challenge,
A gauntlet to be run,
A sport for testing prowess,
A battle to be won.

SATURDAY—JANUARY 11.

MICHEL MONTAIGNE, the 16th century French writer, used to say that there is good in everything if we look for it. Many people complain, he said, of having a bad memory, but he argued that there were advantages even in that:

" One cannot be a good liar; one cannot tell long stories; one forgets offences; and one enjoys places and books a second time round."

Perhaps, after all, there is something to be said for a good " forgetory "!

OYEZ!

Who could refuse
To lend ear to the news,
Rung out each day
In the old-fashioned way?

SUNDAY—JANUARY 12.

BE strong and of a good courage; be not afraid, neither be thou dismayed: for the Lord thy God is with thee whithersoever thou goest.   Joshua 1, 9.

MONDAY—JANUARY 13.

WE all know that often our attitude to things which happen to us makes all the difference, but it helps sometimes to have an actual example to follow.

The late Dr H. E. Fosdick, a well-known American preacher, used such an example in one of his sermons. He pointed out that the writers Lord Byron and Sir Walter Scott were both lame. Byron, he tells us, brooded on his lameness and it made him " sceptical, cynical and savage ".

Walter Scott, on the other hand, ignored his infirmity as far as it was possible to do so, looking for the good and glad and useful occupations, " living a radiant life ".

So, when we are tempted to say, " Ah, but it's different for me . . .", let's remember the only difference is one of attitude.

TUESDAY—JANUARY 14.

WHEN some friends of ours moved house they found in the kitchen a number of things still pinned to the wall—a calendar, some recipes, and this verse:

> *Every grouse shakes this house,*
> *Every grumble makes it crumble,*
> *But loving words and kindly deeds*
> *Will give it all the strength it needs.*

Truly the secret of a happy home.

B

HERE is a smile sent me by Helen Richards Campbell of Kingston, Ontario, in Canada:

He was a very cautious man
Who never romped or played,
He never laughed or ever dreamed
Nor kissed a pretty maid.
So when he passed away they say
Insurance was denied,
For since he never really lived
They claim he never died.

THURSDAY—JANUARY 16.

IT is said that when Leonardo da Vinci was painting his famous picture "The Last Supper", he needed two faces to act as models before he could complete it. One was for the face of our Lord, the other, of Judas.

The artist searched for suitable models, but was unsuccessful. Then one day he saw a young man, a chorister, emerging from a cathedral. The artist was struck with the beauty of the young man's face and he persuaded him to sit as the model for Christ.

Twenty-five years passed and the picture remained unfinished. The face of Judas was still needed; da Vinci had not seen anyone suitable.

Eventually he visited a town 600 miles away and there saw a man with bent back and a lined, haggard face—a tortured face, suitable for Judas. He spoke to the man and persuaded him to act as model. When they entered the building containing the picture, the man remarked, " It's 25 years since I was here last." He had been the model for Christ, but the life he had been leading in the intervening years had changed his appearance into someone fit to portray Judas.

THE FRIENDSHIP BOOK

BELLA had a very beautiful soprano voice—a voice that matched her personality. She went to school in Manchester and later started her musical career.

In the 1920's and 30's when there was much heartrending poverty in the Lancashire towns, concerts were organised to break down the barriers that existed between the employed and unemployed. By this time Bella had become a famous soprano singer and had engagements all over the country; she still found time to take part in these concerts. She was determined to brighten the lives of the people—and she succeeded.

Often a very tired Bella travelled many miles to sing to her Lancashire friends. Showing none of her fatigue she sang their favourite songs, never forgetting her beautiful rendering of " I know that my Redeemer liveth " from Handel's " Messiah ".

Bella—better known as Isobel Baillie—knew that anything that can be done to create harmony is creating happiness.

THE author and philosopher, L. P. Jacks, did most of his work in the days when authors tended to do their writing by hand instead of on a typewriter.

He used to wear the same old jacket when he was writing and years of toil resulted in a badly-frayed sleeve as it rubbed on his desk. He would smile and say, " If ever I get to heaven and St Peter asks me what I have to show for my life, I shall show him this jacket and its sleeve."

He was as proud of that worn sleeve as he was of any single thing he ever wrote.

THE FRIENDSHIP BOOK

THY word is a lamp unto my feet, and a light unto my path.

Psalm 119, 105.

I HAD just finished one job, and, glancing up at the clock, found that I had barely half-an-hour before I was due to go out. " It's not worth starting another job," I said to myself. Then my conscience gave a jerk—for hadn't I said just the same thing only a couple of days ago, and the day before that?

When one comes to add up the time wasted because it doesn't seem worth while starting another job, it is staggering. Perhaps my conscience wouldn't have been jerked into awareness at this time had it not been for the fact that I had just read of a man who learned Spanish, using the half-hour his journey took him to work each day. He was proud of his achievement, and justly so, for he had put those half-hours to a worthwhile use.

I started on the next job . . .

SIR GEORGE SOLTI, the famous conductor, was once asked which instrument he thought was the most difficult to play in an orchestra. He said that he thought it must be the second fiddle, as people willing to play this were certainly the most difficult to find. It was usually easy to get first violins, but the second fiddles were much more difficult.

And then he added this telling thought: " Most of us find it very difficult to play second fiddle. If on the other hand all the second fiddles in an orchestra stopped playing, we would be well and truly sunk!"

NATURE'S BRUSH

Each season has its colour scheme
 —Winter paints hers by night,
Preparing, while we're sleeping,
 Pictures in black and white.

THE FRIENDSHIP BOOK

I KNOW a poet who likes to be known simply as " J. W. " He used to live in London, but moved to a rural district of Sussex where he earns a living working on the land.

" The work I love," he says, " is cultivating the land, raising plants, eating my own vegetables and fruit. Like the rest of the villagers, I grow not only for myself but to give away. This is important—all good country gardeners do it."

To work in order to give away the fruits of your labours. How much happier we should all be if this were our rule of life.

I IMAGINE that at least once in the course of today most of us will make ourselves a " cuppa ", for it is estimated that here in Britain we drink annually an average of 1650 cups of tea each!

So, when you put the kettle on, you might like to recall some of the things which have been said in praise of our national drink.

Prime Minister Gladstone, for instance, said, " If you are cold, tea will warm you; if you are heated it will cool you; if you are depressed it will cheer you; if you are excited it will calm you."

Dr. Samuel Johnson called himself " a hardened and shameless tea-drinker ... who with tea amuses the evening, with tea solaces the midnight, and with tea welcomes the morning."

When the poet Coleridge was asked how many cups of tea he drank, he retorted that he did not count in cups—he counted in *pots!*

Now I'm going to put the kettle on, and sit down and enjoy a " cuppa ". Will you join me?

ST Bartholomew's Hospital, London, is one of the world's great teaching hospitals, yet how many know how it started?

When Henry I was King of England, one of his courtiers, Rahere, was taken very ill while visiting the Continent. He was nursed back to health at the Hospice of the Three Mountains in Italy.

On his recovery, Rahere vowed that he would found a hospital for poor sick folk in London. One night he dreamt that St Bartholomew appeared to him and told him to build his hospital at Smithfield. On his return to England, Rahere visited the King and asked permission to site it on a certain area of marshy ground.

Although King Henry did not think the scheme would be successful, he gave permission and Rahere started work on clearing the land. Before long, neighbouring children asked what he was doing. When he told them, they started to help, and so did other people. Gradually a tiny hospital came into being—only a poor affair by present standards, but the forerunner of the great institution we know today.

SATURDAY—JANUARY 25.

AROUND this time of year in many towns and villages of Scotland, and indeed all over the world, the birthday of Robert Burns is being celebrated.

The life of the poet has been the subject of endless discussion. Nobody knew his failings better than Burns himself. He summed them up in these lines:

God knows I'm no' the man I should be,
Nor am I even the man I could be.

He surely speaks there for every one of us.

THE FRIENDSHIP BOOK

THE Lord is my strength and song, and he is become my salvation.   Exodus 15, 2.

DR BRACKETT was a medical practitioner in the southern parts of the United States. He devoted his life to serving the poor and would travel miles on cold nights to visit needy souls.

He fell in love, but his bride-to-be forsook him on his wedding day because he failed to appear—he had gone to save the life of a Mexican child.

When he died there was a large funeral, but the people couldn't agree on a suitable memorial and one was never erected. Two people, however, did not forget—the parents of that Mexican child. Dr Brackett's surgery had been over a clothing store, so, being too poor to erect a stone themselves, they took the old brass plate from the entrance to the shop and put it on the grave. It simply said:

Dr Brackett
Office Upstairs

A VICAR I know used to preach very short sermons, frequently ending with a few words that people remembered long afterwards. Here are some of his ear-catching words.

" Most people wish to serve God—but only in an advisory capacity."

" When it comes to giving, some people stop at nothing."

" There is no room for God in a man who is full of himself."

HOLD it!" is the traditional expression which photographers are supposed to use when they get just the expression they want from their subjects.

I don't know whether Lord Snowdon uses those words to his distinguished sitters, but he is on record as saying, " It is no good saying, ' Hold it!' to a real moment of life."

How true that is! " Days and moments quickly flying," goes the old hymn. Let us savour the good and glad in every moment as it passes.

THURSDAY—JANUARY 30.

THE French composer Darius Milhaud was once asked, " If you had to spend time on a desert island which of your own music would you take with you?"

He replied, " I wouldn't take any of it. I would take some sheets of blank paper. My favourite composition is always the one I am going to write next."

As the poet Robert Browning said, " The best is yet to be."

FRIDAY—JANUARY 31.

JANET MORRIS, of Maidstone, Kent, sent me a selection of her beautiful thoughts from which I have chosen three:

Life is to know joy through the happiness of others.

We all need to find space, a time to be alone, a time to think, and a time to make our dreams.

Life is to find time to listen, and in so doing, to help and to understand.

FEBRUARY

A N earnest-looking author sat writing in his study—a small octagonal building near Oulton Broad, Suffolk. His home was beautiful and peaceful, but George Borrow had experienced many ups and downs in his life. Some of his adventures had been while acting as a Bible translator in Russia and Spain.

It was his early life he was especially remembering. Always he had wanted to be a success and worked hard to achieve his aim. Now he wanted other people to realise what determination and ambition could do. So in " Lavengro " he wrote: " Let but the will of a human being be turned to one particular object, and it is ten to one that sooner or later he achieves it."

He proved the truth of his statement. So have other famous people. Mrs Harriet Beecher-Stowe, the authoress of " Uncle Tom's Cabin " wrote, " Where persons are determined to be anything they will be."

The more modern Scottish novelist A. J. Cronin, whose books are known all over the world, wrote in his autobiography: " To attain a particular objective one must give everything; offer unsparingly the sum total of one's capabilities."

Vera Brittain would have agreed, for in her book " Testament of Experience " she wrote: " It also proved that if one believed in a purpose sufficiently and persist long enough, achievement will come."

S HEW my ways, O Lord; teach me thy paths.

Psalm 25, 4.

THE FRIENDSHIP BOOK

THESE inspiring lines were published anonymously some years ago:

Take time to think—it is the source of power.

Take time to play—it is the secret of perpetual youth.

Take time to read—it is the fountain of wisdom.

Take time to pray—it is the greatest power on earth.

Take time to love and be loved—it is a God-given privilege.

Take time to laugh—it is the music of the soul.

Take time to give—it is too short a day to be selfish.

Take time to work—it is the price of success.

ONE of the men most feared and hated by Adolf Hitler was Pastor Martin Niemöller, the leader of the Evangelical Church in Germany. To keep him quiet, Niemöller was put in prison. Months later, he was summoned before a special court, and he was suddenly afraid. He had no idea what to expect—and as he was taken along the seemingly endless corridor from the prison cell to the courtroom, he heard a low voice.

As he listened, the voice was quoting, in the Latin version used by the German Catholic Church, a verse from the Book of Proverbs: " Nomen Domini turris fortissima "—" The Name of the Lord is a strong tower. The righteous runneth into it, and is safe."

It was his jailer's voice. We don't know who he was, but what he said dispelled Niemöller's fears and renewed his confidence in God's mercy—from that moment he was never afraid again.

SCHOOL FUN

When it's music time at school,
   That's our favourite time of day,
Instruments are handed out
   And we sing as well as play;
Just the thing for girls and boys,
   (At home we're told to STOP that noise!)

THE FRIENDSHIP BOOK

ON one of our visits to our friend Mary, the conversation turned to the previous Sunday's service at church.

"It was one of the best sermons I have heard from our minister for a long time and that's saying something," said Mary. "You know, Francis," she continued, "the only trouble is that our parson tells us more on a Sunday than we can do on a Monday!"

How right Mary was! But isn't it our ideals, however hard to achieve, that keep us going?

IN the old days in country towns, men seeking employment would assemble at the annual fairs, and farmers would choose the ones they wanted to hire. One farmer was looking for a young lad. He questioned the boys standing in the market place: one could plough, others could milk and clip sheep, but one merely said that he could " sleep well o' nights ". Intrigued, and not a little amused, the farmer hired him.

The boy worked hard, but the farmer was still not certain if he had got a good bargain. Then there came a dark winter night of strong wind and lashing rain. The farmer lay awake worrying about the damage that would be done in the fields. In the morning he looked out and, to his relief, saw that the hayricks were still intact.

At breakfast he told the boy how he had worried all night in case the wind tore the tops off the hayricks.

"I slept soundly," said the boy. "I wasn't worried. *You see, I put them on.*"

THE Dutch Royal family have long been famous for their informality. I like the story of how, when Juliana was queen, on one important state occasion she arranged the photographers in a large semi-circle in the foyer of the hotel where a banquet was being held, telling them that she would call out the guests into a group opposite.

To the photographers' surprise she placed at the centre of their front line a cuckoo clock. She explained, " I want it to be a happy photograph, not everybody looking solemn, so, when we are all ready, pull the trigger and make the bird pop out and do its noise. My guests will all be surprised and laugh. That will be the moment to take your photograph."

WHEN Benjamin Franklin was a boy, he once said to his mother, " I have imbibed an acephalous mollusc."

Thinking he had swallowed something poisonous, his mother made him take a large dose of an emetic. When he had recovered, he confessed that what he had eaten was only an oyster.

His mother gave him a good thrashing for alarming her unnecessarily, and there and then the budding statesman vowed that he would never again use big words when little ones would do.

And he never did!

THEM that honour me I will honour, and they that despise me shall be lightly esteemed.

I Samuel 2, 30.

THE FRIENDSHIP BOOK

THERE is a story which has been repeated often over the years in Finland of a peasant and his wife who were having a hard time trying to wrest some sort of a living from a barren hillside.

So poor were their harvests that for a number of years they had to eke out their flour supply by mixing it with ground bark.

Then one year, their fortune changed and their harvest was good. " Now we can make our bread of rye flour alone, and throw away our bark meal," said the peasant's wife.

Her husband shook his head. " No," he said. " We must still mix our flour and bark. Have you not heard? The frost has destroyed our neighbour's grain."

THE village blacksmith at Briston, Norfolk, in 1699 was a remarkable man. As a hobby he created a unique musical instrument — a cello made of hand-beaten sheet iron with metal strings. It is now in the church at Briston, and I am told that it has a very fine tone. The blacksmith's tune book is there, too, and it bears his name — Clitheroe.

The villagers admired their cellist blacksmith who would sing and play to them in the church, introducing them to all the new hymn tunes of the day. By using his talents in this way he brought happiness to many people in the parish — and so found a marvellous opportunity to serve others.

What a surprise that humble blacksmith would get today if he knew that his cello still gives pleasure to those who visit Briston church. He forged a link that reached down the centuries.

THE FRIENDSHIP BOOK

ANNA GURNEY had often watched from the shore as gales lashed the Norfolk coast near her home. More than once she had seen ships in distress and had watched, sick at heart, as local men tried in vain to get a rope across to people waiting helplessly on a doomed vessel.

When she heard that a Captain Manby was trying to find a method of doing just this she threw herself heart and soul into supporting him. Not only did she give money, she also invited the inventor to experiment by firing the life-saving gun into the branches of a great fir tree at her home. Eventually the new invention, the breeches-buoy, was perfected and has since saved many thousands of lives.

Such activities were unusual for a woman in Victorian days, but that is only half the story. From the time she was a baby, Anna Gurney had had to be wheeled about in an invalid chair. She refused to accept that she was handicapped and insisted on having her chair pulled down to the shore so that she could watch the storms and raise the alarm if she saw any ships in difficulties.

For those who believe that nothing is impossible to those who strive hard enough, Anna Gurney is surely a wonderful example.

LORD SHAFTESBURY, that much-loved champion of the poor and oppressed, once said: " During a long life I have proved that not one kind word ever spoken, not one kind deed ever done, but sooner or later returns to bless the giver, and becomes a chain binding men with golden bands to the throne of God."

ONE of my favourite poets is W. H. Davies, who wrote those famous lines,
> *What is this life if, full of care,*
> *We have no time to stand and stare . . .*

He had a great love for the simple things of Nature and conveyed this in his poems and other writings.

He once said that we measure life in the wrong way—by the number of breaths taken, so that when breathing stops we say life has stopped. He pointed out that real life is measured by *the breaths we do not take*—those " breath-taking moments " as we describe them, moments of wonder, beauty, goodness, gladness, gratitude and glory. It is then we really live!

HOW would you define the word " home "? That question was once asked in a magazine, which later listed the seven best answers received from readers. Here they are:

A world of strife shut out, a world of love shut in.

The place where the small are great and the great are small.

The father's kingdom, the mother's world, and the child's paradise.

The place where we grumble the most and are treated the best.

The centre of our affections, around which our heart's wishes twine.

The place where our stomachs get three square meals daily and our hearts a thousand.

The only place on earth where the faults and failings of humanity are hidden under the sweet mantle of charity.

THE FRIENDSHIP BOOK

INASMUCH as ye have done it unto one of the least of these my brethren, ye have done it unto me.

St Matthew 25, 40.

MANY fall in love, but you don't fall into a happy marriage."

These wise words come from Jean Coggan, wife of the former Archbishop of Canterbury.

She went on: " Togetherness and forgiveness are the things most needed to make a marriage work; you have to learn to forgive quickly and to accept forgiveness."

Simple enough words, but don't they say everything?

IT'S surprising how people will sometimes chase after success without first deciding what it is they are pursuing. Ask any two people what makes success in life and you'll probably get different answers. My favourite definition of success comes from the 19th century writer and philosopher, Ralph Waldo Emerson, who once wrote:

" To laugh often and much; to win the respect of intelligent people and the affection of children; to earn the appreciation of honest critics and endure the betrayal of false friends. To appreciate beauty; to find the best in others; to leave the world a bit better whether by a healthy child, a garden patch or a redeemed social condition; to know that even one life has breathed easier because you have lived. This is to have succeeded."

THE FRIENDSHIP BOOK

GERMAN-BORN Erich Stegmann lost the use of his arms and hands through polio at the age of three. He fought against his disability, never giving in to it. He attended an ordinary school, and came top of the class in painting—holding his brush in his mouth.

Eventually he became internationally known, winning many awards, and managing to support himself through his painting. His own success convinced him that artists similarly disabled would find it easier to market their work collectively. To help them do this he founded the Mouth and Foot Painting Artists Association, which has been such a great inspiration to disabled people. Some of their members were born without hands; others have been crippled by accident. All are united by their love of art and the determination to overcome adversity.

We who are not handicapped owe them a double debt: for the beauty of their paintings and their courageous example.

ABOUT 30 years ago, Marcus Adams, the greatest child photographer of his generation, was speaking at a businessmen's luncheon on his philosophy of life.

" There's a power outside a man," he declared, " and if he can find it for himself, put it into his everyday living, he's a better road sweeper, a better photographer . . .

" Some people find it through faith; some people find it in Nature. Go and sit in a field on a summer's day—and just look at a daisy. If you're not filled with wonder at the power that created *that,* you never will find it."

THE FRIENDSHIP BOOK

FIVE-YEAR-OLD Philip was travelling with his mother in a car when it broke down. Mum got out and examined the engine, then got back in to try it again. She found Philip with his eyes shut, deep in prayer and was just in time to overhear him say, " Please God, help Mum to start this car, and if You can't come send my dad."

I am happy to tell you that the car started without any more bother, so Dad was not needed after all!

IN older times when a jeweller wanted to test the purity and carat value of a piece of gold, he used a touchstone—a stone named basanite. He cleaned the stone, then rubbed the gold across it, leaving a yellow mark. Then he marked the stone with each of several " control " pieces of varying carat gold. As the next step, he put a few drops of acid on the first mark he had made and compared it to the others. Whichever mark it matched determined the carat value. He replied implicitly on his touchstone.

Yes, a touchstone was a valuable testing object—and we have a " touchstone " ourselves—the Book of our Faith. It contains the truths which give us an unchangeable point of reference as we try to sort out the true from the false. Using our touchstone wisely it will test the issues that confront us day by day.

THE Lord seeth not as man seeth: for man looketh on the outward appearance, but the Lord looketh on the heart.   I Samuel 16, 7.

I WANT a good bed that will last," said Grandma, when asked what she would like as an 85th birthday present.

Not for her any cheap rubbish—and when her daughter and family took her to an appropriate shop, she made no bones about telling the young salesman so. She was determined to brighten up her room, and ordered a modern divan.

She was glued to the window when the van arrived with her new purchase, and watched eagerly as it was set up.

"This is a right good bed," she remarked a few days later. In fact she made that same remark scores of times in the years that followed.

Grandma was a mere three weeks short of her centenary when she died peacefully, having enjoyed the comforts of that right good bed a full 14 years!

MANY of us are lovers of hymns and probably have our own favourites, but sometimes when we sing them I suspect we are carried away by the tune and don't always pay the attention we should to the words.

The late Clifford Towlson, a prominent Methodist layman, felt very strongly about this and used to quote this verse:

> *Two Methodist birds in a wood*
> *Sang hymns whenever they could.*
> *They couldn't make out*
> *What they were all about,*
> *But they felt they were doing them good!*

It is a reminder that the words of our hymns do matter.

BARGAIN TIME

THE FRIENDSHIP BOOK

I SUPPOSE there are times when all of us come up against difficult people who are something of a trial to us. When this happens, instead of allowing them to make us impatient and irritated, we might well remember the words of the great preacher, C. H. Spurgeon, who said, in similar circumstances, " They must have been sent into the world, not that I might save their souls, but that they might discipline mine!"

FLORENCE NIGHTINGALE, who achieved so much, once gave this advice: " Live your life while you have it. Life is a splendid gift — there is nothing small about it."

While John Dryden put it in poetry thus:
Happy the man, and happy he alone,
He who can call today his own—
He who, secure within, can say:
Tomorrow do thy worst, for I have lived today.

AS a BBC War Correspondent, Godfrey Talbot went through many grim and dangerous experiences, but in his book, " Permission To Speak " he deliberately plays down these things and emphasises the lighter side. He writes, " There is great sorrow and dark loss enough in the world—and in my own private world—without dilating on tragedy. In any case, one of the blessings of memory is that we tend to fade and relegate the heavy days and harsh encounters, but retain clear and sharp in the mind the occasions that were fun, the entertaining times when we found kindness and success."

MARCH

SATURDAY—MARCH 1.

THIS is how the poet Georgina Hall feels about the coming of Spring:

The smallest hint of wakening Spring and suddenly I see—a promise of the joys to come on every budding tree: the lambs close by their mother's side in green fields all around, nest-building birds creating their own busy, joyous sound.

New joy awaits round every bend, down every leafy lane, new hope and fresh vitality flows through your veins again; it's good to wake from Winter sleep to find that life once more has so much still to offer beyond your open door.

SUNDAY—MARCH 2.

LET the heavens be glad, and let the earth rejoice: and let men say among the nations, The Lord reigneth.   I Chronicles 16, 31.

MONDAY—MARCH 3.

OUR old friend Mary was leafing through her autograph album when the Lady of the House and I visited her the other day.

" Here's a bit of good advice for you, Francis," she smiled.

> *There's a saying old and rusty,*
> *But as good as any new;*
> *'Tis " Never trouble trouble*
> *Till trouble troubles you."*

Well, I don't know whether I looked as if I needed that advice, but it's certainly worth remembering!

THE FRIENDSHIP BOOK

I REMEMBER hearing on the radio years ago in the " Lift Up Your Hearts " programme — that five minutes of help and inspiration — a minister taking as his theme, " What the Papers Didn't Say " in which he listed simple acts of heroism, unselfishness, kindness, goodness which would never make the headlines and yet which were probably far more influential than many of the things which did.

It reminded me of similar words by the late Arthur Mee, best known to us, perhaps, for his " Children's Encyclopaedia ", but who began his career as a newspaper journalist. He said that, unfortunately, " loving your neighbours, suffering long and being kind, working well, hoping all things, enduring all things, cherishing fair play, bearing with fools gladly, thinking no evil, comforting the widow and the orphan, are not news."

In that case, I would rather make " no news " than make news, wouldn't you?

A FRIEND tells me that her church, like many others, has produced a book of recipes supplied by members, to be sold in aid of church funds. It is different from most others, however, for it includes a recipe for Good Looks!

Here is how it goes: " Take five ounces of patience, six ounces of goodwill, a pinch of hope and a bunch of faith. Then take two hands full of industry, a packet of prudence, a few sprays of sympathy, a bowl of humility and a jarful of spirit-of-humour. Season with strong commonsense and simmer gently in a pan of daily content."

A pleasing dish, indeed!

THE FRIENDSHIP BOOK

IN one of her books, Rita F. Snowden tells of a visit she paid to a tiny village school in the Yorkshire Dales where she was able to examine the school's log book going back for nearly one hundred years.

Fascinated, she turned over the pages, reading about the children, their activities, the books they read and poems they learned, the weather, visits into the surrounding countryside, and much else besides.

Then came a change of teacher, and over and over again the pages simply bore the words, " Nothing worthy of notice this week." But of course, it couldn't be true. It wasn't that nothing happened. It was that the teacher didn't notice it!

If ever we feel bored we would do well to remember that little story. If eyes and ears and hearts and imagination are alert, there is always something to notice and to bring interest and colour to life.

MANY readers will have admired the beauty of Royal Worcester porcelain and perhaps visited the works where it is produced. One of the most remarkable pieces to be seen there has none of the delicate colours for which Worcester porcelain is noted. It is plain in colour but the design is raised on the surface.

This is a replica of part of a set made by the 18th century founder of the Worcester porcelain industry, Dr John Wall, for his friend, the Earl of Coventry, who was blinded in an accident. A Braille plate, they call it in the factory—because the Earl could feel the pattern, even though he could not see it. Truly a compassionate and understanding expression of friendship.

PHILLIPS BROOKS was a well-known American preacher in his day. Once, on a visit to England, he was called upon to preach before Queen Victoria.

Afterwards, an English clergyman remarked to the preacher about his calm and poise. " I am afraid I should have been overcome with nervousness in similar circumstances. Didn't you feel at all disturbed?"

" Not at all," said Brooks. " Why should I? I have preached before my mother."

HONOUR thy father and thy mother: that thy days may be long upon the land which the Lord thy God giveth thee.   Exodus 20, 12.

RECENTLY the Lady of the House and I attended the marriage service of two young friends of ours and I was very impressed by the brief, simple but moving address which the minister gave.

He reminded Jack and Barbara how often the word " give " had been used in the service. Barbara, in time-honoured fashion, had been " given away " by her father; each of them gave a ring to the other, and each in their declaration had said, " I give thee my troth."

" All through this service," said the minister, " we have been talking about giving. I ask you to take this word as the rule of your life together—giving, and forgiving."

A rule of life, indeed, not just for brides and bridegrooms but for all of us.

THE FRIENDSHIP BOOK

HOW we look forward to the Spring in all its beauty and freshness after the hard, cold days of Winter! Here is a thought about springtime which struck me very forcefully when I read it in Rumer Godden's novel, " Kingfishers Catch Fire ".

In the book she describes what it is like to live in a chalet high up on a Kashmir mountainside—cut off by snow in the Winter, but glorious in the Spring.

" But to see the Spring," she writes, " really to see it, you must have lived through the Winter first."

This is true not only of the Spring. For do we really appreciate to the full the blessings and beauties of life till we have experienced something of its hardness, too?

JEAN WADDELL is remembered as one of the Anglican missionaries imprisoned in Iran for about nine months in 1980-81. For some reason unknown to her, she was shot, then a few weeks later was arrested and spent several weeks in a detention centre, three of them in solitary confinement.

Throughout her imprisonment, her attitude was always, " Love your enemies, pray for them, and perhaps one day they will play their part in bringing peace and order and justice to Iran."

Most people, when released from such an ordeal, would never dream of going back again. Miss Waddell, a Scot, is made of sterner stuff. Her one wish was to return to the Middle East to continue bearing her witness for Jesus—if not in Iran then some other part of that turbulent area. She ascribed her release and the fact that she was still alive to the prayers of her friends throughout the world.

MARY was busy making marmalade for the church's Easter Sale when we visited her.

"This is my way of keeping Lent," she smiled. "There isn't really a great deal I can give up for Lent, so I thought I would *take* up something instead. In any case, when I *give* something up it may help me—but if I *take* something up it may help someone else."

There won't be many better sermons preached anywhere this Lent than that one.

I AM always impressed when I hear how famous statesmen, authors, artists, musicians, sportsmen and other famous people have reacted to immense difficulties.

After being thrown out of office in 1916, Sir Winston Churchill (then plain Mr Churchill) said he felt like a fish landed on a river bank "gasping for water". Unlike a fish, he did not expire, but took up painting. It was an interest which consoled him through many dark patches in his political career, and continued even after he became a famous politician.

The novelist Howard Spring tells how as a small boy he read and remembered a sundial's inscription: "I count only the hours that shine." In later life he realised the "gold" that could be "mined from the dark rocks of adversity and how foolish and frivolous life would be if it consisted only of sunshine."

Truly we learn by our misfortunes and are stronger because of them. As a once popular song used to put it, the thing to do after receiving a knock is to "Pick yourself up, dust yourself down and start all over again."

SATURDAY—MARCH 15.

LAST week, the minister gave out the number of the children's hymn. Sixty or so children at the Sunday morning service happily sang " There's a Friend for little children ".

Modern critics of religious music might hold up horror-struck hands at this Victorian hymn, but everyone at that crowded service seemed to enjoy it.

How surprised Albert Michlane would be to know that the words he wrote for his Sunday School scholars over 120 years ago are still sung by children all over the world!

He was an ironmonger with a shop in Newport, Isle of Wight. One Saturday evening, after a busy day in the store, he sat down to put into simple words the message that Jesus could be the children's greatest friend. It was hard work—in fact it took him nearly all night.

His reward was the way the children liked the hymn. It was published in December, 1859, and quickly became popular. As I heard last Sunday, they still love to sing it!

SUNDAY—MARCH 16.

THOU wilt shew me the path of life: in thy presence is fulness of joy; at thy right hand there are pleasures for evermore. Psalm 16, 11.

MONDAY—MARCH 17.

CHARLES KINGSLEY, the novelist, once advised: " Never lose an opportunity of seeing anything beautiful. Welcome it in every fair face, every fair sky, every fair flower, and thank Him for it, Who is the foundation of all loveliness."

OLD WARRIOR

Long ago she sailed the seas,
High and proud in the salty breeze.

TUESDAY—MARCH 18.

WHEN, over 50 years ago, the Rev. Bernard Heywood was appointed Bishop of Ely, his congregation at Leeds Parish Church were saddened to lose him. A few older parishioners still remember these words he spoke in his farewell sermon: " If you will bury me in your hearts and come each week to put a few fresh prayers upon the place, I shall never be able to find words in which to thank you."

Who can doubt that his new work was greatly enhanced by the memories and prayers of his people? To remember and to be remembered—what happiness this brings!

WEDNESDAY—MARCH 19.

I HEARD the story of a man who wanted to go to the village of Mathons. Driving along, he came to a crossroad, and saw a signpost which said it was four miles to Mathons one way and seven to Croxley the other.

Taking the Mathons road, he drove four miles, but no village came into sight. Seeing a man working in a cottage garden, he stopped. " I am on the right road for Mathons, amn't I?" he called.

" Depends which way you go," replied the man. " If you keeps going the way yon car's heading, you'll get to Croxley. But if you turns her round, and goes back t'other way, you'll get to Mathons in about eight miles."

" But," exclaimed the traveller, " the signpost at the crossroads said Mathons was four miles *this* way."

" Maybe so," grinned the man, " but you mustn't take any notice o' that thing—he twirls with the wind, he does!"

IS there anything more lovely and inspiring than a new baby? Here is how Edward Borland Ramsay responded to a birth in the family:

O new-born babe, we welcome you
Into this wilting world of ours;
And with your coming, sense anew
The freshness of the summer flowers.

This living miracle of birth
Has filled our hearts with joy and love—
So pure, it seems that all the earth
Reflects the grace of God above.

So we commit you to His care,
As we were done by long ago,
In continuity of prayer,
Unbroken in its hallowed flow.

THERE is an old story of a man who dreamed he was walking along the beach with Jesus, and across the sky flashed scenes from his past life. He saw two sets of footprints in the sand — his own and those of Jesus.

As the last scenes of his life flashed before him he noticed there was now only one set of footprints. He also realised he had come to the lowest and saddest times of his life.

He turned to Jesus and said, " Lord, you said that once I decided to follow you, you'd walk with me all the way. But I've noticed that during the worst times of my life, there is only one set of footprints."

" Yes," said Jesus. " That was when I was carrying you."

D

SATURDAY—MARCH 22.

THE Lady of the House and I called on old Sandy the other evening. He was just sealing an envelope when we went in and he grinned at us. " I'm going to India!"

" India?" we said. " Well, not really *going*," he laughed. " I'm sending a little contribution to an Indian appeal fund."

Then he told us how the sermon at church the previous Sunday had been about " Influence " and the minister had quoted a verse by Anna E. Hamilton:

This learned I from the shadow of a tree,
That to and fro did sway against a wall,
Our shadow selves, our influence, may fall
Where we ourselves can never be.

" So," said Sandy, " I thought I'd like to ' go ' to India—and perhaps a few other places as well, when I can afford it."

Perhaps we could join him!

SUNDAY—MARCH 23.

AND when the hour was come, he sat down, and the twelve apostles with him.

St Luke 22, 14.

MONDAY—MARCH 24.

THERE is an old saying, " There are three things that cannot be recalled—a spent arrow, a spoken word and a lost opportunity." That last word reminds me of a saying of which a friend of mine is very fond: " The trouble with opportunities is that they always look much better going than coming!"

Don't let one go by today.

THE FRIENDSHIP BOOK

IT was some time since the Lady of the House had seen Marjorie, and when she called she found her friend had a new dog—a large mongrel called Buster.

Marjorie was, in fact, eating her dinner, and put it down on a low table while she talked.

" Mind Buster doesn't eat it," warned the Lady of the House.

" Oh, Buster won't touch it," came the confident reply. " I've been taking him to dog training classes. He'll only take it if I say ' Buster, take!' "

At that, Buster finished off her dinner in two gulps.

BOOKS of sermons are not as common or as popular as once they were, but I was recently looking through a book of sermons by Dr H. E. Fosdick who was for many years the minister of the Riverside Church, New York.

In his introduction to the book, Dr Fosdick explains what he feels to be the true nature of a sermon. " It should," he says, " get things done, then and there, in the lives and minds of the audience."

This reminded me of a story of a theological student who was summoned to the College Principal's study. The Principal sat there with the student's latest sermon. In frosty silence he glanced from the sermon to the student and back again to the sermon.

At last the student could bear it no longer and he burst out, " It will do, sir, won't it?"

" It will do *what*?" asked the Principal.

Wasn't that exactly Dr Fosdick's point? And isn't it true of *lives* as well as sermons? What do they *do?*

THE FRIENDSHIP BOOK

MRS GEORGINA HALL of Coppice, Oldham, has written many beautiful poems. This one she sent me is called " Hiker's Heaven ".

The long road stretches far ahead—a silver ribbon
  winding,
The view around, above, below, enchantingly
  spellbinding,
The open sky, the lonely moor, the village in the
  hollow,
These are the ways my wandering footsteps always
  love to follow.

Through every season, green or gold, cold Winter's
  mantle white,
The countryside in all its moods breathes wonder
  and delight;
I count my blessings every day that I have eyes to
  see
The wealth of beauty heaven bestowed for humble
  folk like me.

SIR JAMES SIMPSON, the discoverer of chloroform, was once asked by an interviewer, " What do you consider was your greatest discovery?"

The questioner expected that Sir James would say, " Chloroform," but instead the great scientist replied, " My greatest was when I discovered that Jesus Christ was my Saviour."

On this Good Friday, many will give thanks that they too made that discovery for themselves, and perhaps others will be led to it.

OFF WE GO

The lessons we learn when we are young
Stay with us all our days
—Harmony, good sense and constant care
Help ease life's roughest ways.

THE FRIENDSHIP BOOK

O NE of the outstanding actors of the great days of the cinema was Lionel Barrymore. In 1936 he broke his hip and the fracture never healed. Most people thought that would be the end of his acting days—but not Lionel Barrymore. He used the setback as a means to even greater acting triumphs.

For nearly 20 years, although in constant pain, he played dozens of successful parts from his wheelchair, showing how great is the power of the human spirit to triumph over adversity.

H E is not here: for he is risen, as he said. Come, see the place where the Lord lay.

St Matthew 28, 6.

S T PAUL reminded the Corinthian Christians that " faith, hope, and love abide ". We hear quite a lot about faith, and rather more about love, but perhaps not such a lot about hope.

Do you know this little verse by Oliver Goldsmith, author of " The Vicar of Wakefield "?

Hope like the gleaming taper's light adorns and cheers our way,
And still as darker grows the night,
Emits a brighter ray.

The humorist Douglas Jerrold once remarked that " In all the wedding cake, hope is the sweetest of the plums ", whilst the novelist Victor Hugo said that " the word which God has written on the brow of every man is hope ". Yes, hope is every man's encourager especially at Easter.

APRIL

TUESDAY—APRIL 1.

ALAN GRICE was a dairy farmer in the Lancashire town of Rainford. Day by day, without fail, he made an early morning delivery of milk to housewives.

But Alan Grice did more than that. He also cultivated flowers — and with the advent of Springtime, he delivered something else along with the milk. Each customer on his milk round received a little bunch of daffodils — with Alan's compliments.

A small gift, but how much pleasure it must have brought!

WEDNESDAY—APRIL 2.

THIS amusing poem was sent me by Irene Bernaerts of Tarring, Worthing.

The beds are made, the kitchen gleams,
The hall is shiny bright;
The windows sparkle as they should
To let in all the light.
There's not a single magazine
Left lying anywhere,
No sewing basket on the floor,
No knitting on the chair.
I wish my friends would visit me,
They would be most impressed
And say that as a housewife
I'm a cut above the rest.
But when the place is in a mess
And nothing's straight at all,
Then that's the day my friends will choose
To pay a social call!

THE FRIENDSHIP BOOK

SURELY one of the happiest things in family life is the bond of affection that so often unites a young boy and his grandfather. Where this is found the difference in age simply doesn't matter.

Dr David Owen, the well-known politician, remembers how, when he was five or six, he would go out cycling with his grandfather. He would perch on the crossbar and steer and grandfather would pedal, and together they would explore the countryside round their home in Wales, where his grandfather was a minister.

Perhaps somebody reading this has done much the same as young David or his grandfather. But few can have done *exactly* the same for, you see, David's grandfather had been blind from birth!

It's a lovely example of the trust that can exist between young and old.

WALTER DE LA MARE wrote some delightful poems. " Jim Jay " may not be his best as *poetry,* but what a lot just three brief lines of it have to say to us:

> *Poor Jim Jay*
> *Got stuck fast*
> *In Yesterday.*

We all know people like that, don't we—people who wish they could have their time over again, or who go on regretting something which happened in the past, or who are always complaining that " things are not what they were ". They, like Poor Jim Jay, are stuck fast in Yesterday.

Let's pull ourselves loose and escape to all the blessings of Today!

SATURDAY—APRIL 5.

A NUMBER of years ago, Mr Raymond Ashworth was the conductor of the Hebden Royd and Hepton Over-Sixties Choir, based at the now popular tourist centre of Hebden Bridge, West Yorkshire.

He recalled how, on one occasion, after the choir had competed in a contest with Dvorak's " Going Home ", one of the oldest members said to him, " That ' Going Home ' were grand. It were so lovely I just had to stop and listen while we were singing it."

Relating the incident afterwards, Mr Ashworth said, with a smile, " I'm very glad all the other members didn't show their appreciation in the same way!"

SUNDAY—APRIL 6.

G O ye into all the world, and preach the gospel to every creature.   St Mark 16, 15.

MONDAY—APRIL 7.

J OSIAH WEDGWOOD, the great potter and founder of the famous firm, was once badly injured in an accident. Instead of bemoaning his fate, he began to take a keener interest in ornamental pottery—an interest that greatly enriched his life and that of his firm.

Another man with a different disability was James Thurber. When he visited Sir Compton Mackenzie in Scotland, the latter wrote: " His courage in bearing his blindness is an inspiration. If ever I become blind I shall try to be as brave as Thurber."

These two are just examples. There are similar ones around us in everyday life—people who in spite of disability really live their lives.

TUESDAY—APRIL 8.

WHAT is the magic contained in a smile? Even the most surly person often cannot help but respond to a smile from a friend or neighbour. We are all touched by the shy smile of a young child, or the gleeful smile of a baby at the sight of its mother.

Romantic novelists have long used the power that lies in a sweet smile to help their heroines snare their loved ones. The gracious smile of our Queen has been responsible for much of her popularity. While the mysterious smile of the " Mona Lisa " has intrigued throughout the ages.

Scientists inform us coldly that a smile is merely the movement of 13 muscles, while a frown, it seems, requires 50 muscles. But the fact remains that a frown is very depressing while the small amount of effort to produce a smile works wonders.

WEDNESDAY—APRIL 9.

THE philosopher, George Santayana, was lecturing one glorious Spring morning when he suddenly broke off in the middle of a sentence, saying, " Gentlemen, I am afraid that sentence will never be finished. I have an appointment with April." And he gathered his papers together, left the lecture theatre and went off into the country!

Of course, Santayana was a bit of an eccentric and it is perhaps as well that most of us don't and can't act on an impulse of that sort and drop everything.

All the same, perhaps there are *some* things which, on a lovely Spring morning, we *could* leave till later, and keep an appointment with April in all its freshness and beauty, if only by walking round the garden or standing at the open door to savour the glory of the day.

CLOISTERS

THE FRIENDSHIP BOOK

AN all-too-little-known book which came out of World War II was " Poems From The Desert ". It consisted of verses written by soldiers of the British Eighth Army. One of the most moving was " A Soldier—His Prayer " which was scribbled on a scrap of paper found in a trench in Tunisia.

Stay with me God, the night is dark,
The night is cold: my little spark
Of courage dies. The night is long:
Be with me God, and make me strong.

I imagine that there are many other places besides a battlefield where that unknown hero's heart-felt prayer might be of help and comfort to countless numbers of us.

RECENTLY, the Lady of the House and I were invited for a meal at the home of two friends, Ewart and Jane. I have noticed before that Ewart never fails to give a word of appreciation to his wife for an excellent dinner. This time he did it by reciting a verse of Meredith's:

We may live without poetry, music and art,
We may live without conscience and live without heart,
We may live without friends, we may live without books,
But civilised man cannot live without cooks!

Well, I am sure that neither the poet nor Ewart really believes the first three lines of that verse. But how good it is to hear someone give a word of appreciation for something as basic as a well-cooked meal. So often, I am afraid, we tend to take it all for granted.

THE FRIENDSHIP BOOK

I WONDER if you have noticed that some church clocks have blue faces with gold figures and hands. This used to be much commoner than now. Indeed, it is said that Henry VIII made a decree that the faces of church clocks should be " blew, and the signs upon them gilte." It is thought that the choice of these colours may have had something to do with the fact that they were the colours of the vestments of Aaron and his sons mentioned in the book of Exodus.

But whatever the history or legend behind all this, I must confess I love these bright clock faces. Sometimes we say " time flies," on other occasions that " time drags," but I like to think of time as a bright, glad gift which brings joy in its use, the " shining hour," as it has been called.

G OD is our refuge and strength, a very pleasant help in trouble.   Psalm 46, 1.

H AVE you heard of this inscription from the 7th century, discovered in India?

" Jesus, blessed be His Name, has said: ' This world is a bridge. Pass over it, but do not build a house on it.' "

We do not live in this world for ever. New Testament writers suggest we are like strangers and pilgrims on the earth.

It is tempting to confine our attention and our interests to this world, but when this life reaches its end, the world will be seen to have been just a bridge into God's eternity.

THE FRIENDSHIP BOOK

A LITTLE boy from Glasgow was visiting a country farm and watched the cows being milked. Then he saw the calves being fed with milk from buckets. He commented excitedly: " I see it all now! They get it when they are wee and have to give it back when they're big!"

MRS Frances Grattan of New Brunswick, Canada, wrote me a letter which I quote with her permission.

" We had new next door neighbours and somehow had managed to get off on the wrong foot with them. Soon after they'd moved in they'd had a bonfire which blew smoke over on to my washing. Maybe I spoke a bit more sharply than I intended. Anyway, after that, all our attempts to be friendly were met with rebuffs and we were sad. We'd been good friends with our previous neighbours. And being older folk, the goodwill of those around us meant a great deal.

" The other day, though, we were just getting home when the young man from next door pulled up in his car, jumped out and rushed up to us. His face was red, his hair standing on end. ' I've got to tell you,' he cried excitedly. ' Lorna—my wife—has just had an 8 lb baby girl! I can't believe it's happened at last! Isn't it marvellous?'

" It was indeed marvellous, their first child and long awaited, we learned. We showered congratulations on him and next day I went out to buy a special gift to take in to mother and baby. Now, instead of two new friends we have three! And they've even asked us to be godparents. Sometimes problems are solved in the nicest possible way."

THE FRIENDSHIP BOOK

I SUPPOSE everybody has heard of Helen Keller, but how many people know of Anne Sullivan? It was Anne, a 20-year-old student, who believed that she could teach the sad little girl deprived of speech, sight and hearing and whose matchless patience and understanding brought about that first great triumph—the day when her pupil realised she had a name and was called Helen Keller.

That was only the beginning, of course, but it was under Anne's tutorship that Helen Keller ultimately graduated at Radcliffe College with honours in four languages, and a sound knowledge of economics, philosophy and literature.

Of course, Anne Sullivan could have done little without Helen's courage and determination. But what would Helen have done without Anne's patience and dedication?

M ARGARET RILEY, who lives near Wooler, Northumberland, echoes the feelings of many in these lines:

From mansion to cottage,
From semi to flat,
From penthouse to bedsit,
The answer is—that
No matter the country,
No matter the place,
No matter your colour,
There's one common base.
It's the comfort around you,
It's the things that you own,
It's the room you relax in,
That place you call home.

THE FRIENDSHIP BOOK

AN old farmer was building a wall in his farmyard and was being chaffed by one of his cronies who happened to be passing.

" That wall's not right straight, George," he said.

" Ah, well," said George after a moment, having surveyed his handiwork, " Everything's different nowadays. Even string isn't as straight as it used to be!"

WATCH and pray, that ye enter not into temptation: the spirit indeed is willing, but the flesh is weak.   St Matthew 26, 41.

A TASK which seems impossible at a distance somehow becomes possible when we have to face it.

Robert Falcon Scott found himself famous when he returned from his successful Antarctic expedition in 1904. Requests for him to give lectures on his adventures flooded in, but he shrank from the prospect. He had found it much easier to battle with glaciers in the Antarctic than to stand in front of an audience and give a lecture!

However, he forced himself to accept the invitations. And when the time came and he stood before a sea of faces, he suddenly found himself speaking confidently about his experiences in the land of ice and snow. He made people feel that it had been the best fun in the world.

Scott proved that what seems impossible can, with faith and resolution, be done, and be done well.

TREASURE

In scenery where mountains loom
We thrill to grandeur all around,
But in a single, modest bloom
Beauty's perfection may be found.

E

THE FRIENDSHIP BOOK

DURING a break in a mid-week church meeting the chairman announced, " The organ will now play." There was silence. The organist sat stolidly at his instrument. After a pause the chairman tried again, but this time he said, " Mr Best will now play the organ."

Those near enough saw the organist's features relax as much as to say, " That's better!" and he started to play.

Was the organist being a bit difficult? Perhaps; but he certainly had a point. Organs don't play themselves and books don't write themselves, and trains don't drive themselves; indeed, most of the things we enjoy depend on *someone* who makes our enjoyment possible. It is only right to give them credit for what they do.

ELIZABETH and her husband William had been married a dozen years when they went on holiday to the little Welsh village of Ffestiniog. Here their ten-year-old son Willie contracted scarlet fever from which he died.

The death of her only son left his mother shattered. She didn't know what to do with herself—until her husband advised her to write down her feelings and experiences, and get it out of her system that way.

As she wrote, the pain began to diminish, and in 1848 was published her book, " Mary Barton ", a story about the lives of cotton workers in Manchester. This was the first of several successful novels written by Mrs Elizabeth Gaskell, who is perhaps best known for her second work, " Cranford ".

THE FRIENDSHIP BOOK

VISITORS to lovely Keswick in the Lake District may call in at St John's Church. Among the many names associated with this fine building is that of the Rev. Frederick Myers who in 1838 was appointed perpetual curate of this newly-formed parish. He is still remembered for the library he founded and for his encouragement in education.

He is remembered for some of his sayings, too. Wise remarks like these:

" A man who does his duty and who reverences his conscience so greatly that, to preserve it unharmed, he will face any difficulty and submit to any penalty—he is a great man."

" Not in the things that are done for us, but in the things that are done *by* us, does our strength lie."

DO you know where sheepdogs are mentioned in the Bible? I didn't, until I heard about them through a little boy.

Jimmy had been listening to his mother reading the 23rd Psalm just before he went to bed. When she had finished he said, " That's a story about a shepherd, but there's nothing about his dogs. He must have had dogs, mustn't he?"

Jimmy went off to bed still worrying about the dogs. In the morning the first thing he said was, " The shepherd had two dogs and I know their names."

" You do?" said Mother.

" Yes," said Jimmy, " it says in the psalm: ' Goodness and Mercy shall follow me all the days of my life '. So, if they followed the shepherd *they* must have been his dogs, mustn't they?"

SEA MURMURS

SATURDAY—APRIL 26.

JOSEPH BILLIO . . . if you think there is something familiar about that name, you are right.

When Billio went to be a minister at the Congregational chapel in Maldon, Essex, in the 17th century, he was the first nonconformist minister to work there.

Life was certainly not easy for him, but we are told that Joseph worked hard for his people and the good of his cause. In fact, he worked so hard and so enthusiastically that today we still use the saying, " to work like Billio ".

What a good way to be remembered!

SUNDAY—APRIL 27.

BLESSED are they that dwell in thy house: they will be still praising thee.   Psalm 84, 4.

MONDAY—APRIL 28.

THE human spirit rising above sadness and adversity is one of the miracles of life. Handel's " Messiah " has been said to be the greatest inspirational music ever written, but the circumstances in which it was written, as recorded by one of his biographers, are an even greater inspiration.

" His health and his fortunes had reached the lowest ebb. His right side had become paralysed and his money was gone. His creditors seized him and threatened him with imprisonment. For a brief time he was tempted to give up the fight. But then he rebounded again to compose the greatest of his inspirations, the epic ' Messiah '."

THE FRIENDSHIP BOOK

MRS C. ROBERTS of Walsall wrote this lovely poem which captures the feelings of many a parent at a daughter's wedding. She calls it " Father's Pride ".

Today she looks so beautiful
She takes my breath away.
I look at her in wonderment,
Not knowing what to say.
Sophisticated lady she,
Yet still a little girl to me.
I can't believe today will be
My daughter's wedding day.

Today she looks so wonderful,
So confident and gay.
Yet through my tears I still can see
A little girl at play.
Soon she will leave this house that's been
Her home from birth to seventeen.
My child-bride daughter, she's a queen
On this, her wedding day.

THE Rev. Samuel Proctor was addressing the Caribbean Conference of Churches in November 1981:

" God's power among men is not as visible as big cars—it is a mother teaching her child to pray. It is not in submarines and ships of war—it is Mother Teresa soothing the brow of a starved and dying Calcutta woman. It is not so much in the display of royalty getting married—as in a Harlem rehabilitation centre, where one lost sheep is trying to find its way back to the fold."

MAY

THURSDAY—MAY 1.

IN the 1930's they nicknamed Glenn Cunningham, the American track runner, "The Kansas Flyer". He repeatedly broke national and world records for the mile, and in 1936 won an Olympic Silver Medal.

In any circumstances this would have been a great achievement, but when Glenn was a boy he had been badly injured in a fire. Doctors said he would never walk again.

But he did! He learned to walk by holding the handles of a plough to support himself and following it across a field. Little by little he developed his mobility and strength until eventually he became one of the greatest runners of his generation . . . a tribute to the resilience of the human spirit when faced with difficulty and handicap.

FRIDAY—MAY 2.

I WAS tired, and more than a bit irritated when roused from slumber by the sound of a dog barking. Then I looked out of the window—and I saw the most beautiful sunrise.

"The heavens declare the glory of God, and the firmament showeth his handywork," said the Psalmist. I agree—I saw it for myself that morning.

Isn't it true that we are so often engrossed in mundane matters that we miss some of the beauties of God's creation? No artist's brush could have done justice to the beautiful sunrise on which I was able to feast my eyes that May morning. And if that dog hadn't rudely awakened me, I'd have missed it!

IN THE WOODLAND

Only last month a carpet of russet
   Crackled and rustled beneath gaunt trees,
But now, transformation and new life awakening:
   Happy the traveller whose haunts are these.
Through every season, every mood,
There's magic in a bluebell wood.

AN old friend of ours, now in her 70's, recently emigrated to New Zealand to be with her daughter there. She was able to take very few of her possessions but she insisted on taking an old vase. " I have been looking at that on my mantelpiece for over 50 years and I want to go on looking at it!" she said.

Changes come to us all but to hold on to at least *something* familiar seems to give us roots. I am sure Adeline Whitney felt this when she wrote:

God does not send strange flowers every year.
When the Spring wind blows o'er the pleasant
places,
The same dear things lift up the same fair faces,
The violet is here.

THOU art Peter, and upon this rock I will build my church.   St Matthew 16, 18.

THE American writer Kenneth Krueger said, in one of his articles, " When I was a six-year-old boy my playmates told me that if I walked on the cracks on the side-walk (pavement) it would bring me bad luck. For weeks I had my eyes glued to the cracks as I minced my steps to and from school. I did not see the beauty of the May flowers. The singing of the robins and the meadow larks were silenced because of my pre-occupation with this childish fear."

Childish, indeed; yet how many of us rob ourselves of the joys about us through foolish and groundless fears? Let's learn the love of things and people and life itself which casts out fear.

IN May 1849, three ladies arrived in York. Two were quite healthy, but the third looked very ill. Indeed it was to try to regain her health that the journey was being made. She hoped for recovery; her companions feared otherwise. Their destination was Scarborough, but at the invalid's desire they spent a little time in lovely old York.

The visitors were Charlotte and Anne Brontë and their friend, Ellen Nussey. One of Anne's delights on a previous visit was to see the Minster and she wanted to go back and see it once more.

Years later, Ellen Nussey wrote: " Her visit to York Minster was an overwhelming pleasure, not for its own imposing and impressive grandeur only, but because it brought to her susceptible nature a vital sense of the greatness of Our Divine Architect."

Anne's favourite motto was: " To aim high is all that matters; even if one fails, God would recognise the intention."

A motto that can inspire us still, well over 100 years later.

THE German poet, Rainer Maria Rilke, wrote in her book, " The Journal of My Other Self ": " Her smile was not meant to be seen by anyone and served its whole purpose just in being smiled." An odd thought?

But don't we all have our " secret smiles "? Smiles at some pleasure we enjoy, some beauty we behold, some thought that flits through our mind, some sound we hear—the song of a bird or a tune on the radio.

Why *not* smile to ourselves? There is such a lot to smile about!

THE FRIENDSHIP BOOK

I WAS listening to a gardener on the radio talking about the history of roses. He pointed out that one of the most prolific periods in their development was just after World War II.

He suggested that one possible reason for this was the impulse, after years of destruction and darkness, for people to surround themselves with as much beauty as they could.

Whether or not we accept his theory there is little doubt that beauty can be an antidote to feelings of gloom . . . flowers, pictures, bright colours can all help to dispel the darkness and make this world a better place to live in.

POSSIBLY one of the most popular hymns ever written is " Stand up, stand up for Jesus " but I wonder how many people know how it originated?

Last century, a noted evangelist and opponent of slavery in America was the Rev. Dudley Tyng. He took a leading part in the religious revival of 1858 centred on Philadelphia. Shortly after a great meeting he was fatally injured by a piece of farm machinery. As he lay dying, he expressed a wish to send a message to the Prayer Meeting of the Philadelphia YMCA. " Tell them," he said, " to stand up for Jesus."

This so impressed a friend of his, the Rev. George Duffield, that he set to work to write a hymn on the theme and it was read, a short time later, at the memorial service for Dudley Tyng. Duffield had no intention of wider circulation for the hymn, but it created such an impression that it was not long before it had gone round the world.

WISE FOREFATHERS

There must have been a time when someone said,
  " This is the very place to settle down,"
And others, envying them their choice,
  Came too and built a sturdy market town.

Fulfilling as it did their every need,
   An air of quiet contentment still remains.
Beyond the motorway, perhaps, a different world,
   But here a peaceful river, leafy lanes.

SATURDAY—MAY 10.

MABEL LUCIE ATTWELL was born in 1879 in Mile End, London. As a small girl she loved to sketch and when she was older her family encouraged her to go to art school. She soon showed that she had very original ideas—she sketched fairies, goblins and dimpled children.

However, when she tried to sell her work, agents did not like it and persistently refused to help her. With dogged determination Mabel kept on trying, and at last an agent took some of her work, not because he liked it, but because he simply wanted to encourage her.

No one was more surprised than he when her style started to attract attention. The demand grew and she was asked to illustrate many of the well-loved fairy tales of the day. The public took to its heart what she had it in her to express and she became the first successful woman artist in this country.

SUNDAY—MAY 11.

A WISE son maketh a glad father.

Proverbs 10, 1.

MONDAY—MAY 12.

IN her book, " The Country Child ", Alison Uttley tells how Susan Garland guiltily turned back two miles on her way home from school just to pick up a crust she had carelessly dropped.

Perhaps this Christian Aid Week, when the annual appeal is being made for hungry, homeless and deprived people, some feeling of guilt may not be inappropriate for all of us as we give what we can and " live more simply, that others may simply live."

THE FRIENDSHIP BOOK

IF we ourselves are " getting on in years " as the saying goes, or want to give a bit of help to someone who is, we may find the following lovely verses useful. They are by Mrs Thomas Ellis Baker who wrote under the name Karle Wilson and she called her poem " Old Lace ".

Let me grow lovely growing old,
So many fine things do—
Laces and ivory and gold
And silks need not be new.

There is healing in old trees,
Old streets a glamour hold.
Why may not I, as well as these,
Grow lovely, growing old?

RECENTLY, a friend of ours planned a short holiday and, not wanting to travel very far afield, chose a hotel in a little village about 20 miles from where she lived.

She made friends with some other people staying in the hotel who told her that they were planning to go on a " mystery tour " run by the local coach proprietor, so she decided to join them.

As the scenery grew more and more familiar she realised what was happening. The " mystery tour " was to her own home town!

" But would you believe it," she said, " I have lived here most of my life, and they took me to places I had never seen before!"

Of course there is a lot to be said for seeing new places and doing new things—but what a lot we often miss close at hand.

THE FRIENDSHIP BOOK

ANNIE HIGSON was schoolmistress at Burston, Norfolk, in 1914. Her pupils came from poor homes and she did all she could to help them. When they had leaking boots, she bought them new ones. Finding them very intelligent, she introduced them to French and typewriting as well as normal lessons.

Local landowners distrusted her " fancy ways " and they dismissed her. This upset the parents, who at once refused to send their children back to school unless she was there. Annie told the children to come to her on the village green and she would teach them there.

News of her outdoor classes spread all over the country. People collected money so that she could start a school of her own—a school of freedom, love and justice. It is still used today and is a memorial to Annie, the woman who helped not only the village children of Burston, but brought the attention of the country to all poor village children.

Annie Higson did her duty—and was given the strength to carry it out.

ONE of the most brilliant and admired Secretary-Generals of the United Nations was the Swede, the late Dag Hammarskjöld. He had long been in the habit of jotting down his thoughts about life, and after his death a collection of these was made from the manuscript he had left.

One of these random thoughts is well worth remembering if we come face to face with difficulties we think we cannot overcome: " Never measure the height of a mountain till you have reached the top; then you will see how low it was."

THE FRIENDSHIP BOOK

IN an interview Barbara Kelly, the TV personality, and her interviewer seemed a little confused about her age. After a bit of calculation they decided she was 52. " Really," she said, " I thought I was 53. Is that all I am? Well, frankly, I don't spend too much time looking back. My favourite age is where I am at. I can't even remember being 51."

That's a few years ago now, but I reckon Barbara Kelly will go on feeling like that all her life. It is her way of looking at age—and one we might all well share.

THE Lord be between me and thee, and between my seed and thy seed for ever.

I Samuel 20, 42.

IN 1781, an anonymous Colchester clergyman made a tour of parts of England and wrote an account of his impressions. Describing one scene, he wrote, " I shall remember it and thank God for it as long as I live. I am sorry I did not think to say grace after it. Are we to be grateful for nothing but beef and pudding; to thank God for food and not for happiness?"

Well, sadly, even the traditional " grace before meat " has largely fallen into disuse, but how right was that unknown clergyman to remind us how much there is besides food for which we might at least say a silent " grace "—natural beauty, sunlight, refreshing rain, holidays, friends, books, music, the smile of a little child. Thank God for happiness!

HAVE you ever examined closely Millet's famous painting, " The Angelus "? A friend pointed out to me recently something that I confess I had never noticed before.

The young man in the picture appears to be fiddling rather self-consciously with his hat, but the girl is clasping her hands in prayer and standing with bowed head.

One might have expected her to be picked out by the rays of the setting sun which the artist has painted. But, no. Instead, the light falls on the wheelbarrow and the tools the two have been using. It is a lovely way of reminding us that to work is to pray. Even the humblest work is beautiful in God's eyes.

WEDNESDAY—MAY 21.

I LIKE this definition of a grandmother, written by a boy of eight:

" A grandmother is a woman who has no children of her own and therefore loves boys and girls of other people. Grandmothers have nothing to do; they only have to be there. If they take us for a walk they go slowly past beautiful leaves and caterpillars. They never say ' Come along quickly ', or ' Hurry up for goodness sake '. They are usually fat, but not too fat to tie up our shoelaces. They wear spectacles and sometimes take out their teeth. They can answer every question such as why dogs hate cats and why God is not married. When they read to us they do not leave anything out, and they do not mind if it is always the same story. Everyone should try to have a grandmother. They are the only adults who always have plenty of time. "

NURSES have often been called "ministering angels" and their ministry often extends to the mental and spiritual needs of patients as well the physical.

I heard of someone recently who was having a pretty tough time in hospital, not only through considerable pain and weakness but through anxiety about his future and about his family. One day he said to a nurse, " I feel as though I am up against a brick wall."

The nurse put her hand on his arm and said gently, " No, you're not up against a brick wall—you are just in a tunnel."

It's a thought that may help many of us in darkness—keep watching for the gleam of light in the distance.

FRIDAY—MAY 23.

THESE three inspiring verses are from the pen of the Scottish poet, Edward Borland Ramsay:

Think not of tomorrow and what it may bring:
Rejoicing or sorrow, come Winter or Spring;
The days and the seasons are God's to command—
Think not of tomorrow, but trust in His hand.

Think not of tomorrow and what you shall eat:
God's harvest is plenty, His promise complete,
The sheaves of His mercy still offer you bread—
Think not of tomorrow, God's banquet is spread.

Think not of tomorrow, and what you shall wear:
The rose and the lily, He fashioned with care;
Much more does He love you, the days going by—
Think not of tomorrow, God's grace will supply.

BISHOP CORBETT of Norwich in the 17th century was an unconventional figure—" not a bit like a bishop " some people said, recalling his fondness for practical jokes.

But he was remembered, too, for his great kindness to people in need, including those of other religions than his own.

It is said that on one occasion he was dining in an inn when he happened to look out of the window and saw in the street an old, shabby ballad-seller trying to sing the songs he had for sale in such a weak, quavering, croaky voice that passers-by simply laughed at him, leaving the poor man in tears.

Immediately the bishop left his meal and ran into the street where he began to sing the songs in his strong, cheerful voice, attracting so many customers that very soon the old man had sold out his copies. Then with an encouraging pat on the ballad-seller's shoulder the bishop went back to finish his dinner.

SUNDAY—MAY 25.

SO the last shall be first, and the first last: for many are called, but few chosen.   St Matthew 20, 16.

MONDAY—MAY 26.

BILLY, the young nipper along the road, has scored off me again, much to his delight. I was in the garden as he passed on his way home from school.

" Mr Gay," he called out, " Do you know that heat travels faster than cold?"

" Well, er . . ." I began.

" It does, you know," he said. " Anyone can catch cold!" And he was off—as quick as heat itself!

THE FRIENDSHIP BOOK

SOME time ago I took a walk in the country with a naturalist friend and I was amazed at the sounds of bird and animal and insect to which, through his sensitive ear, he was able to draw my attention.

Then towards us came a couple of teenagers with a transistor blaring away! When they had passed, my friend said, " You know, that reminds me of the guide who was showing a party of visitors the Niagara Falls. He called out, ' And now, ladies and gentlemen, if you will stop talking for a moment you will be able to hear the mighty roar of the Falls! ' "

I think we all could listen more than we do sometimes, to the sounds of the natural world.

PERHAPS when worries tend to keep us awake at night it might help us to recall the story of Bulstrode Whitelock who was British Ambassador to the Hague in the 17th century.

One night he was tossing restlessly in bed, anxious about the problems of his work and his country. An old servant heard him and approached: " Sir, may I ask you a question?"

" Certainly," replied the Ambassador.

" Did God govern the world before you came into it?"

" Undoubtedly," was the reply.

" And will He govern the world when you have gone out of it?"

" Undoubtedly."

" Then, sir, can you not trust Him to govern the world while you are in it?"

The tired Ambassador turned on his side and fell fast asleep.

GIVE AND TAKE

There's nothing like a tasty bite to eat
To make a friendship perfect and complete.

THE FRIENDSHIP BOOK

GRANDPA," asked a small girl, " Will heaven be as nice as Cleckheaton?"

Perhaps you wonder what could possibly be the connection between heaven and a rather grimy Yorkshire mill town, but for the little girl in question Cleckheaton was the place where she spent occasional holidays with her grandfather, where there were all kinds of special treats, and where she always had great fun.

How grateful we should be for everyone and everything which helps to make for us " a heaven on earth."

COMPLIMENTS that are genuine are worth giving, but those that are given just to flatter or to gain friendship or support are what the poet Tennyson called " the clink of tinsel ".

The best advice for anyone paying a compliment that I ever heard was, " Never pay a compliment as if you expected a receipt!"

I LIKE these anonymous lines sent me by a reader in America:

A little more kindness, a little less creed,
A little more giving, a little less greed,
A little more smile, a little less frown,
A little less kicking a man when he's down,
A little more ' we ', and a little less ' I ',
A little more laugh, a little less cry,
A little more flowers on the pathway of life,
And fewer on graves at the end of the strife.

JUNE

SUNDAY—JUNE 1.

THE earth is the Lord's, and the fulness thereof;
the world, and they that dwell therein.

Psalm 24, 1.

MONDAY—JUNE 2.

A YOUNG mother I know graduated in psychology, but she tells me that the other day she learnt a lesson from her little son, Timothy.

She had been working in the kitchen when she heard the sound of shattering glass and rushed out into the garden to find Timothy standing before a broken window.

" Young man," she said, " go and phone your father and tell him just what you have done."

" Hello, Dad," he said timidly into the phone. " I was playing with my ball, and you know the big window in the lounge—well, Dad, I've just broken the little one next to it."

TUESDAY—JUNE 3.

IN his delightful book about village life in East Anglia, " Akenfield ", Ronald Blythe tells the story of Duncan Campbell who was a farmer all his life.

Duncan talks lovingly of tending the land. " I add fertiliser to the good natural humus of the grass and freshen it all up with irrigation. The rule with land is to give—then you can take."

A good rule for land, as Duncan says. And a good rule, too, for the whole of life.

THE FRIENDSHIP BOOK

IS there any value in dust? Most of us—or housewives at any rate—probably grumble about the way it accumulates. However, the sisters at the Holy Cross priory at Heathfield in Sussex found a way of turning their dust into money. They collected the contents of their vacuum cleaner and sent it to a major drugs company which turned it into an anti-allergy vaccine.

So dust can be good for you after all!

RECENTLY I had occasion to walk along a narrow street of drab terraced houses with doors opening directly onto the pavement. No trees, no grass, no colour, just grey dreariness, until suddenly my eyes were caught and held by a window-box full of plants at an upper-storey window—red and pink geraniums and bright blue lobelia. I stopped to admire it, and a woman passing nodded—" Looks real festive, doesn't it?" she said. " Belongs to Mrs Jones. She's bedridden. It's something bright for her to look at."

" Did she put it there herself?" I asked.

The woman laughed. " No, as a matter of fact we had a whip round in the road, bought the wood and plants, and a couple of the boys fixed it up.

" You see, Mrs Jones has been what you might call a real good neighbour all her life, always ready to help, or to listen to other people's troubles, so when she became bedridden we thought we'd like to do something special to cheer her up. Only," she added, with a beaming smile, " the funny thing is that although we did it to cheer *her* up, it brightens up the whole road and us as well!"

THE FRIENDSHIP BOOK

I REMEMBER as a boy, as probably many of my readers will, masses of scarlet poppies growing in fields of yellow corn. Weed-killers and other modern methods of farming have made that almost a thing of the past.

However, we can still have poppies in our gardens—among them the lovely Shirley poppies in reds and pinks and whites. We owe them to the Rev. William Wilks, vicar of Shirley, who in the summer of 1880 discovered, among the poppies which had invaded his garden from the neighbouring cornfield, one flower edged with white. He saved the seeds and next year, out of several hundred plants, had a handful with the same unusual white edge. Year after year he went patiently on with his selective breeding till he achieved the results we know today.

When I look at my Shirley poppies I try to remember not only William Wilks, but a whole multitude of people, who by tireless labour have achieved for us much that we take for granted.

I HAVE mentioned before the interest and inspiration which can come from browsing through old autograph albums which were once so popular.

In several such albums I have come across a verse whose author seems unidentified, but his (or her) words must have brought encouragement to many who read them:

Life is mostly froth and bubble;
Two things stand like stone—
Kindness in another's trouble,
Courage in your own.

THE FRIENDSHIP BOOK

COME unto me, all ye that labour and are heavy laden, and I will give you rest.

St Matthew 11, 28.

AT the end of an inspiring address, the Bishop told the young reporter who had been eagerly recording everything that had been said: " When you write this up, I would appreciate your not mentioning the several anecdotes I related—you see, I may want to use them again in other speeches ".

The reporter duly obliged, for he wrote: " The bishop told several stories which I cannot repeat here."

IN the quaintly-named Last Drop Village near Bolton in Lancashire, there is a fascinating clock museum with dozens of old timepieces of all shapes and sizes including many graceful grandfather clocks.

It was there that the Lady of the House and I came upon the following words written many years ago by an American and placed inside his much-loved grandfather clock: " You dominated our parlour, standing, as you did, much taller than any of the human occupants of the house . . . you were a friend to all, a regulator of the speed of our lives and a faithful link between a generation now gone and a generation yet to come . . . You were the voice of my home."

Since I read these lines, our own more humble clock has taken on a new meaning as a reminder of the precious and wonderful gift of time.

THE FRIENDSHIP BOOK

THE engineers who built the M5 motorway in Devon did a marvellous job. It is most impressive, but you know the bit I like best? Not far from Exeter is a little tunnel one foot wide below the motorway. Its purpose? To help the badgers cross safely from one side to the other.

THIS charming poem, " Cottage for Sale," is by Mrs B.D.P. Jemison of Bridlington.

Weeds now crowd the flagstoned path
That winds towards the cottage door,
Before the porch, a rustic arch
That once a gown of roses wore.

Against the time-worn mellowed walls
The overladen lilac leans,
Loose on its hinges hangs the gate,
And through the pear tree sunlight streams.

There's lichen on the pantiled roof
Where watchful latticed windows lean;
Their cobwebbed panes like watchful eyes
Look sadly on the garden scene.

And from a stalwart apple tree
Hangs some forgotten child's old swing,
While on the trellised cottage wall
Sweet pea and " morning glory " cling.

Upon a freshly-painted board
Where roses and honeysuckle trail,
There, written large for all to see,
These magic words " Cottage for Sale ".

QUIET WAYS

Who would not be happy,
Contented with their lot,
With home an old-world cottage
In some secluded spot?
Not for them the worried frowns
Of folk who live in busy towns.

THE FRIENDSHIP BOOK

I LIKE this story of a coward who became a hero.

Charlie Coward was a British sergeant-major who, during World War II, was captured and sent to prisoner-of-war camps and labour camps. He escaped several times, but was always caught. He was never afraid to stand up for the rights of his fellow-prisoners and bluffed his way out of many a difficult situation.

When he was interned in a labour camp not far from the dreaded concentration camp at Auschwitz, he received a plea for help from some of the prisoners. He wormed his way out of the labour camp and into Auschwitz, and by making certain arrangements with folk in charge, he helped over 400 Jewish people to freedom at great personal risk to himself.

Many folk today are still grateful for his courageous exploits in helping them to escape. In fact there is, in Jerusalem, an Avenue of Righteous Gentiles—named in honour of those who, at risk to their own lives, helped the Jews during the Nazi regime.

One plaque bears the name of Charlie Coward, the cheerful cockney sergeant-major who, although Coward by name, was anything but a coward in character.

ONE of the ancient Greek gods was Aeolus, God of the Winds, and there used to be a Greek custom of stretching wires between the towers of a castle so that when the winds blew, music was made. They called it an aeolian harp.

They created music from the storm, beauty from turmoil.

THE FRIENDSHIP BOOK

B E ye strong therefore, and let not your hands be
weak: for your work shall be rewarded.

II Chronicles 15, 7.

S OME " Wayside Pulpit Wisdom " passed to me by
a friend who keeps an eye open for these things:
" If you suffer from a long-standing, deep-seated
trouble—try kneeling!"

T HIS poem by Barbara Malik will be appreciated
by those of us lucky enough to have a granny.
She calls it " Granny's Hands ".

They were hands that hard work had moulded,
And care and worry had lined;
They were gnarled and knotted and wrinkled,
From many long years of grind.

They were hands that once had been shapely,
With fingers long and slim,
But the scars they bore showed a life of chore,
And a struggle hard and grim.

They were hands that helped the needy,
The sick and ill at ease;
They were hands that were always ready
To try to serve and please.

They were hands that got things accomplished,
No task was too great or too small.
With a grip of determination,
Granny's hands tackled them all.

THE FRIENDSHIP BOOK

THE Lady of the House was telling me about a young friend of hers who was taken to see a waterfall for the first time in his life. Tony stood fascinated as the torrent of water poured down over the rocks. Eventually his father said, " Come on, Tony, we really must be getting back to the car."

But Tony tugged at his father's hand and pleaded, " No, Daddy. Let's wait till it has stopped!"

HE can say what he likes. I will be a musician. I won't be a lawyer." So decided young George Frederick Handel for the umpteenth time. George was born on 23rd February, 1685. Ever since he could remember, his father, Surgeon-Barber Herr Handel, had discouraged George's interest in music. He had even taken George from a school where his musical ability had been recognised and encouraged.

Herr Handel did not realise that every night, when the household was asleep, the boy practised very, very softly on an old spinet in the attic.

One day George wistfully watched his father set out to attend the Duke of Saxe-Weissenfels. If only *he* could meet the musical Duke, too. On impulse, he ran behind the carriage trying to keep out of sight. But his father saw him, and stopped the carriage. Now for it, thought George. To his amazement, Herr Handel merely said " Come along," and ushered him in beside him. Impressed by the boy's initiative and determination he had given in at last.

He took the boy to meet the Duke, thus beginning Handel's strong link with the Duke and his musical family— a link that led to special tuition and eventually to his becoming a great composer.

FRIDAY—JUNE 20.

A PARISH magazine in Kent told of a minister who cut his sermon short, explaining that his dog had eaten part of his sermon.

The moment the service was over, a stranger to the church rushed up and asked if the minister's dog had any pups. " If so, I would like to give one to *my* minister," he explained.

SATURDAY—JUNE 21.

A FRIEND of mine has told me how he learned to stop worrying—something I am sure many of us would like to do!

He became so depressed about his constant worrying that he sought the advice of someone in whom he felt he could confide.

" I'm afraid I am a worrying type," he said to his confidant. " I seem to worry about everything."

" You do?" was the reply, " What are you worrying about at the moment?" My friend told him.

" And what were you worrying about yesterday?" Again he received a reply, but the questioner persisted, " And what were you worrying about last week?"

This time there was a long pause, and at length my friend said, " I can't remember."

" Then it couldn't have been very important, could it?"

It suddenly dawned on my friend that most of the things he worried about *weren't* very important—were quite forgettable, in fact! Worry had simply become a habit and he decided there and then to break it. Of course, it took a bit of effort, but once he recognised his worry for what it was he soon found relief from it. Worth trying, isn't it?

G

THE FRIENDSHIP BOOK

GIVE us this day our daily bread.

St Matthew 6, 11.

IF they give me the money I'll stand on the monument myself instead of them bothering with a statue."

The speaker was Gioacchino Antonio Rossini, one of Italy's most famous composers. He was not being ungrateful when he heard that the people of his native town Pesaro were proposing to launch a public appeal to erect a statue in his honour. He was just being his usual humorous self.

His music is full of happiness and joy. For the first 37 years of his life he wrote almost as many operas. Some are now forgotten, others like " The Barber of Seville " (1816) and " William Tell " are still popular.

Rossini often poked fun at his own methods of composing, once telling an admirer that he had composed " William Tell " when out fishing. On another occasion he advised a young composer, " Nothing primes inspiration more than necessity whether it be the presence of a copyist waiting for your work or the prodding of an impresario tearing his hair."

Apart from the joy his music brings, one lesson he has left is how much happiness can be achieved by not taking oneself too seriously.

FOR wisdom in a very few words I like the Chinese proverb: " Keep a green bough in thy heart and God will surely send thee a singing bird."

WEDNESDAY—JUNE 25.

IN his book, " Word Power—Life Power " Vernon Howard tells of someone who jotted down in a small note-book what he called " beautiful " words. They included such words as crystal, blossom, graceful, sparkle, melody, dove, harmony, joy, love, ideal, peaceful, and many, many others—a list to which he was constantly adding.

Each morning he would read through a dozen or so on his list, pondering them quietly for a moment or two, determining that, when the opportunity arose, he would use some of them in his conversation during the day.

He told a friend, " Because I looked at the world only through rose-coloured words I became rose-coloured myself!"

THURSDAY—JUNE 26.

I REMEMBER a minister telling about conducting a service in a church where he had not been before. Everyone was sitting towards the back of the church so just before the sermon he suggested it might be better if they came nearer the front.

Everyone did this except three people sitting together in the back pew. The minister proceeded with his sermon but couldn't help feeling that the three might have followed the lead of the rest of the congregation.

However, after the service he went to the door, pausing to speak to the three as passed. He then discovered that one of them was a severe cripple who would have had great difficulty in getting to church at all but for the help of the other two.

How important it is to be sure of our facts before we make our judgments on other people!

MORNING BREAK

FRIDAY—JUNE 27.

"IF you can't be kind, be quiet, that's what I tell my family," a young woman said standing at a bus-stop recently. " It's what my mother used to drill into me."

Her friend nodded: " Good advice, but not always easy, especially if you've a short temper as I have."

Just an ordinary sort of conversation in a friendly village, but it set me thinking.

It brought to mind Dr Samuel Johnson, the famous 18th century dictionary compiler and author, who said on one occasion: " Getting money is not all a man's business; to cultivate kindness is a valuable part of the business of life." He would not always find this easy, for he was a man who knew his own mind and delighted to speak it, though sometimes, it is recorded, he was sorry afterwards for what he had said.

Tolerance comes into this, too, for if one tries to be truly tolerant, then it is easier to be kind. Joyce Grenfell, the well-known actress and author, who died a few years ago, once gave her opinion on tolerance: " I hold it to be a beautiful quality when it is the outcome of love and understanding. Tolerance means loving in spite of imperfection!"

SATURDAY—JUNE 28.

A FRIEND from Yorkshire sends me a delightful story clipped from a local newspaper of a man driving through the Dales and passing a farm with the notice: " NEW LAID EGGS ". A little farther on, not to be out-done, another farmer advertised: " FRESH NEW LAID EGGS ". But a third beat them both with his claim: " EGGS NOW BEING LAID "!

THE FRIENDSHIP BOOK

THOUGH I walk through the valley of the shadow of death, I will fear no evil: for thou art with me.
Psalm 23, 4.

FOR over 20 years in the middle of last century, Dr Walter Farquhar Hook was the Vicar of Leeds. He did great work among the poor of the city and had a special interest in industrial conditions and in education. He supervised the building of at least 30 schools and 21 churches, as well as the rebuilding of the parish church itself.

Into this new building he invited, as special preacher, George Doane, the American bishop of New Jersey, who gave an address on Baptism. At the end, he made an appeal to anyone not baptised to come forward, but no-one responded.

Some months later, a young man called on Dr Hook in the vestry. " You won't know me, sir," he said, " but some time ago I was passing your church and saw that an American bishop was going to preach, and though I was never one for churchgoing it was a bad day and I thought I'd go in out of the cold and see what a Yankee bishop looked like."

" Ah, yes," said Dr Hook, " I remember the occasion. The bishop was very disappointed that no-one answered his appeal about baptism and he went away feeling his visit had been a failure."

" Not at all!" said the young man. " I listened to every word and though I didn't go forward then, I have since been baptised and confirmed. That service changed my life."

When we speak of success and failure, how little we often know about the results of our actions.

JULY

TUESDAY—JULY 1.

MRS TAYLOR of Foster, Quebec, Canada, tells me these lines were found on a piece of paper in a restaurant in Montreal. The poem was titled " The Art of Living ":

> *To touch the cup with eager lips and taste, not drain it;*
> *To woo and tempt and count a bliss, and not attain it;*
> *To fondle and caress a joy, yet hold it lightly,*
> *Lest it become necessity and cling too tightly;*
> *To watch the sunset in the west without regretting;*
> *To hail its advent in the east, the night forgetting;*
> *To smother care in happiness, and grief in laughter;*
> *To hold the present close, not questioning the hereafter;*
> *To have enough to share, to know the joy of giving;*
> *To thrill with all the sweets of life—that's living.*

WEDNESDAY—JULY 2.

THE Superintendent of a children's home sent one of her girls to buy some plums.

" Be sure and pinch one or two to make quite sure they're ripe," she told the little shopper.

The child returned with a triumphant smile and handed over the plums, together with the cash. " There's your money," she said. " Nobody was looking so I just pinched the lot!"

THE FRIENDSHIP BOOK

THE Lady of the House and I were walking in the country recently and fell into conversation with a farmer. Our talk turned to the weather.

" Ah, well," said the farmer. " Some people are never satisfied. It is either too hot or too cold, or too wet or too dry. I know a fellow — if he could have his way he would have it raining on one of his fields and not on the one next to it! Never satisfied!"

I couldn't help feeling that we are all a bit like that at times — and not just about the weather. If there are things that ought to be changed and we can change them, well enough; otherwise, a measure of acceptance and contentment are very necessary parts of life.

ON a visit to London I went to Westminster Abbey. There, in the North Transept, I paused in front of a marble memorial dedicated to Jonas Hanway. My mind did a quick flip back to my school days and I recalled learning that it was Jonas who carried the first umbrella in London.

The memorial makes no reference to this, but reads: " The helpless infant nurtured through his care. The friendless prostitute sheltered and reformed. The hopeless youth rescued from misery and ruin, and trained to serve and defend his country. In one common strain of gratitude they bear testimony to their benefactor's virtue."

We might well wonder for which of his many benevolent works this man, who died in 1786, would be remembered. Oddly enough it is for none of those listed on the tablet. Jonas Hanway is most renowned for giving us the humble umbrella.

SATURDAY—JULY 5.

THE Lady of the House was leaving the grocer's when she heard someone behind her say, " When I was young I used to be frightened of the dark, too. You won't be frightened when you're older."

I pass this on because the Lady of the House assures me that the girl who was receiving the advice was five and the girl who was giving it was—seven!

It seems we're never too young to start handing out advice!

SUNDAY—JULY 6.

HEAVEN and earth shall pass away: but my words shall not pass away.   St Mark 13, 31.

MONDAY—JULY 7.

A MINISTER amused his congregation but also taught them a very valuable lesson in his talk to the children one Sunday. Standing at the foot of the high pulpit he asked, " Is anybody good at jumping?"

Quite a few young hands shot up. " Well," he continued, " Could any of you jump from here up into the pulpit?"

No hands went up this time.

" I can," said the minister, " I'll show you how," and, beginning at the foot of the steps leading to the pulpit, he took a little jump on to the first step. From there he jumped on to the second, and so on till he reached the top! Then he went on to talk to them about things which can only be accomplished step by step, little by little . . . a lesson most of us need at some time or other in our impatience for quick results.

H

THE FRIENDSHIP BOOK

BETWEEN the wars a pedlar, laden with a pack of useful items, was often seen trudging along Yorkshire and Lancashire lanes. Always welcome at lonely farms and cottages he was well known for his cheery outlook and for the rhymes he made up as he walked through the countryside.

There was nothing remarkable about his simple verses, except the optimism, faith and humour they revealed, and the fact that, up to the age of 20, Tom Phillips had experienced great difficulty in learning to read and write.

His verses grew popular and eventually a little booklet of the works of Tom the Pedlar was published. Here is an example of his homely wisdom:

To every man is given a mind
 To find some thing which others miss;
When found, as was by God designed,
 He tells to others what it is.
Go, seek those things which you alone
 May find, and straightway make them known.

I SUPPOSE we all have moods and states of mind when we don't like ourselves very much — anger, depression, irritability and so on.

J. B. Priestley, the playwright and author, had some rather unusual advice to give in such situations. " Try to regard your states of minds as *visits to places*. Now I am in the angry place or the melancholy place, or the misunderstood-by-everybody place. If you do this, you don't identify yourself with these states of mind: they are not *you*. It really works."

I must try that!

THE FRIENDSHIP BOOK

HAPPINESS—true happiness—is so important to us all that whenever I come across a definition of it which is new to me I jot it down on a special page of one of my notebooks.

Here is the latest addition to that page. It was said by Dr. Norman Vincent Peale whose books such as " The Power of Positive Thinking " and " A Guide to Confident Living " have brought inspiration to millions of people. Asked about happiness, he said, " He is the happiest man who thinks the happiest thoughts."

I think that is hard to beat!

CONISTON, in Cumbria, is a lovely village. It was there that Arthur Ransome, the author of children's books such as " Swallows and Amazons " and " Swallowfield," spent many happy times. His stories full of fishing and sailing lore were based on his own experiences.

Arthur Ransome was born on 18th January 1884, and wanted to be a writer from an early age, but his parents and friends tried to persuade him to do other work.

In fact, it was not until he stayed with his friends, Mr and Mrs W. G. Collingwood at Coniston, that he received real encouragement to make writing his life's work. Instead of being depressed at his failure to achieve success with writing he was uplifted and cheered by the Collingwoods' faith in his future as a writer and their steady encouragement.

Later he wrote that " the rest of my life has been happier because of them ".

Good friends indeed.

THE FRIENDSHIP BOOK

THE writer Henry van Dyke wrote this little verse:
Let me but live my life from year to year,
  With forward face and unreluctant soul;
  Not hurrying to, nor turning from the goal,
Nor mourning for the things that disappear
In the dim past, nor holding back in fear
    From what the future veils, but with a whole
    And happy heart, that pays its toll
To youth and age, and travels on with cheer.

LET the words of my mouth, and the meditation of my heart, be acceptable in thy sight, O Lord.

Psalm 19, 14.

I WAS interested in the comment of the owner of a garden who was showing a television expert round it during a programme. He said, " I think successful gardening is very much a matter of contrast: contrast in colour, contrast in size of plants."

We all have our own ideas about gardens, but that remark reminded me of a prayer I once heard in which the minister thanked God for what he called " the alternating mercies of life " — for day and night, for work and leisure, for times of solitude and times of company, for joys that make us glad and sorrows that discipline us, for successes which inspire us and failures which make us humble.

How dull life would be if there were no contrasts in it! Variety, as the old saying goes, is indeed the spice of life.

THE other day I stopped to chat to a neighbour who was busily weeding her garden.

"This is the worst part of gardening, Mrs Brook, isn't it?" I said.

"Well, actually, I don't think so," was her reply. "There are so many bad things in the world that I have no power to get rid of, but I *can* pull up weeds and feel I am doing at least a little to make the world more beautiful."

Think of that next time you are weeding or simply tidying up. I know I will.

A RATHER sad-looking man hurried into the bedroom of a sick little girl. At once he began to make her smile by reciting a poem to her.

Nothing very original about that! Many parents, aunts, uncles and friends make up stories and verses to entertain children. Yet not many have recited what was to become one of the best-loved nonsense poems in the world, "The Owl and the Pussycat went to sea . . ." for that is what Edward Lear made up for Janet, the daughter of friends.

It was not the first of his verses, for he had already written, illustrated and published "Nonsense Rhymes" and "More Nonsense Rhymes" at his own expense.

His life was a constant fight with ill-health, career "ups and downs" and disappointed hopes. Born in 1812 in London, he had hoped to be a successful artist and worked hard to this end but he was only moderately successful. His real gift was in making up the delightful nonsense verses that have enchanted children—and adults—the world over.

LITTLE FINGERS

The wish to be in tune with life
*   Is central to the human heart;*
To learn the way to harmony,
*   No child need be too young to start.*

FRED the carter was an ordinary farm labourer. He was nearly blind, having got some lime in his eyes when he was young, but he could still plough as straight as a gun barrel.

He also showed me the easy way of carrying out each job, not because he was lazy, but because if you take a steady pace and do the job correctly, you achieve much more without becoming exhausted. He insisted that I learn to use a prong left-handed as well as right-handed, thus making it so much easier to get at awkward corners in the dung-yard or on top of a rick.

He lived close to the earth and had a simple faith—belief in the seed time and the harvest, an understanding of Nature, a love of children, his fellow men and animals.

I take my hat off to Fred the carter. This wise old chap was content to do his best, not for the boss or for a wage packet, but for the land and the countryside he loved.

FRIDAY—JULY 18.

CLOCK CAPERS " is the title Miriam Eker has given this amusing poem.

> *The clock has stopped, I thought it best*
> *To let it have a little rest.*
> *But when I tried to make it go,*
> *Alas, its progress was too slow!*
> *I wound it up, and moved it round,*
> *But still it did not make a sound!*
> *And then there came into my mind*
> *(A stranger thought you could not find)*
> *I slapped it hard—it did the trick—*
> *My precious clock began to tick!*

SATURDAY—JULY 19.

SEVERAL years ago I knew a middle-aged woman who often used to say, " Oh, I do hope I grow old gracefully." I am sure she did, and she was not alone in her wish. In Cornwall there is a motto carved on one of the stones leading to ancient St Just-in-Roseland church which reads: " Grow lovely growing old ".

Easy to advise, but hard to accomplish. Yet people who have had the most trouble, sorrow and sickness in their lives often seem to accomplish it best.

I once saw this prayer printed on cards in St Sampson's Centre for Older People in York.

Almighty God, who made each day to be lived to the full,

Please bless all older people.

Give us all that we need for friendship, comfort and leisure;

Above all give us true joy living one day at a time,

Freed from anxieties, with peace in our hearts

Trusting in Jesus Christ, Our Lord, Amen.

SUNDAY—JULY 20.

WHERE two or three are gathered together in my name, there am I in the midst of them.

St Matthew 18, 20.

MONDAY—JULY 21.

ONE day, when President Abraham Lincoln of the United States was walking down a street, someone commented, " He's very common-looking."

President Lincoln overheard the remark and replied, " Friend, the Lord prefers common-looking people; that is the reason He makes so many of us."

THE FRIENDSHIP BOOK

IF children can sometimes be exasperating, they can also be wonderful! The journalist Monica Furlong tells a story which illustrates both points I think.

One cold night she was awakened out of a sound sleep by the call of her three-year-old son. She ran down the chilly corridor to his room where he was sitting up in bed. He flung his arms round her and said, " Mummy, I'm your friend!"

" He had just thought of it!" said Monica. And even at three o'clock in the morning he had to tell her.

I think it was worth getting up to hear, don't you?

IF the great French scientist Louis Pasteur had been asked in later life what creature he liked best, he might have replied, " The silkworm."

The reason for such a reply would have been that in 1865 he was asked to carry out an investigation into the death of silkworms. These industrious little creatures provided the thread that played such a big part in France's economy, and they were dying in thousands.

After much hard thinking, observation and work, Pasteur decided that the silkworms were suffering from a disease caused by a very tiny germ.

People ridiculed his theory. Whoever heard such a stupid idea? The man must be mad. But Pasteur was proved right. He not only discovered the cause of many ailments, he produced remedies for them.

Nowadays he is remembered as the founder of the Institute in France that bears his name, but it was those tiny creatures, the fragile silkworms, who first helped him to become famous.

THURSDAY—JULY 24.

I LIKE these lines from George Bernard Shaw's play, " Pygmalion ":

" The great secret, Eliza, is not having bad manners or good manners, or any other particular sort of manners, but having the same manners for all human souls. In short, believing as if you were in Heaven where there are no third-class carriages, and one soul is as good as another."

FRIDAY—JULY 25.

HAVE you heard the parable of the two seas? I found it in a book, " The Meaning of Service ", by the well-known American preacher, Dr Harry Emerson Fosdick. He wrote: " The Sea of Galilee and the Dead Sea are made up of the same water. The Sea of Galilee makes beauty out of it, for the Sea of Galilee has an outlet—it gets to give. It gathers in its riches that it may pour them out again to fertilise the Jordan Plain.

" The Dead Sea has no outlet. It gets to keep."

SATURDAY—JULY 26.

WHEN the great, kind and generous actor Kenneth More died in 1982, many impressive tributes to him appeared in the newspapers.

" He had fine capabilities, he was a master of his craft and in 1956 he won a Picturegoer Gold Medal," said one theatre critic.

His old friend Emlyn Williams said simply, " He always turned up on time, he knew his part, and he did it extremely well."

I suspect it was the tribute Kenneth More would have appreciated most.

SUNDAY—JULY 27.

B E not thou far from me, O Lord: O my strength, haste thee to help me. Psalm 22, 19.

MONDAY—JULY 28.

I KNOW a very good cook who is also a bit of a philosopher. Here is her recipe for a good start to the day:

Take a portion of Scripture and season with prayer. Sprinkle in a few kind thoughts and sweeten with happy memories.

She says that if you get the mix right, the lovely flavour will last you all the day through.

TUESDAY—JULY 29.

A S the Prince and Princess of Wales continue their married partnership, I am sure they often think back to their wedding day in 1981 and the multitude of wedding gifts they received.

I wonder which pleased them most? The one designed by the King of Tonga? Or the one made by his Queen? Or maybe the grandmother clock constructed by a blind and disabled Londoner? After all, 1981 was the International Year of the Disabled, as well as the year of the Royal Wedding.

But I have a feeling that maybe the one that pleased the royal couple most was the humble gift from a Sussex lass named Mandy Brooks. Her gift was a set of table mats which she had embroidered herself. Each stitch had taken her 20 minutes, for Mandy suffers from spina bifida, which hampers her movements. Her wedding gift represented hours and hours of loving, painstaking, and no doubt at times painful industry.

THEN AND NOW

Age-old monuments they stand,
The great cathedrals of our land,
Bearing witness still today
As first when pilgrims came to pray.

Beauty, grandeur unsurpassed,
Built for worship, built to last,
Pointers in an age of strife
To the finer things in life.

THE FRIENDSHIP BOOK

CYRUS FIELD dreamed that he would one day lay a telegraph cable under the Atlantic and so improve world communications. He had a driving will-power and with his engineer brother he formed a deep-sea telegraph company.

He sailed to Newfoundland to start the work, but it was not as easy as he expected. For 12 years he tried and failed, suffering one setback after another. The ocean itself seemed to be against him when the cable broke just after engineers in Newfoundland and Ireland had seen a spark, and at one time he was on the verge of bankruptcy. People were unwilling to lend him money to be lost at the bottom of the sea.

It seemed impossible that Cyrus would keep trying, but he did, and on 29th July 1866, after a last strenuous effort the cable was successfully laid. Two hemispheres were joined by a length of wire.

IN 1983, the World Council of Churches held its Sixth Assembly in Vancouver with 3000 delegates from all over the world. You can imagine something of the planning which must have gone into these meetings—about travel, discussions and worship, business sessions, language difficulties and hospitality.

But a detail which didn't seem to get into most of the Press reports was that the Canadian women had made 3000 embroidered cushions for delegates to place on their hard seats in the vast marquee!

I wonder whether those present may not remember that delightful touch long after they have forgotten some of the theological discussions. Little things do count!

AUGUST

FRIDAY—AUGUST 1.

A N ancient country custom which has been revived in some places in recent years is that of Lammas Day (August 1st), a name which derives from two Anglo-Saxon words meaning " loaf " and " mass ". It was the custom on this day to offer thanks by bringing to church a loaf of bread made from the first of the new season's corn—the first fruits of harvest.

While harvest-time looks back gratefully to a crop safely gathered in, Lammastide looks forward hopefully to that which is to come. How important it is, not only in the matter of harvest and of our food, but of so much else in life, that we should give thanks not only for what we have received, but, in the words of a familiar grace, " that which we are about to receive "—the gladness of anticipation.

SATURDAY—AUGUST 2.

B ENJAMIN DISRAELI once commented that " the secret of success in life is for a man to be ready for his opportunity when it comes ". Whilst Ralph Waldo Emerson said that " no great man ever complains of lack of opportunity ".

That reminded me of the South African writer, Alan Paton, who remarked that " no one is too weak, too vile, too unimportant, to be God's instrument ".

The hymnist John Keble advised anyone overcome by feelings of melancholy or self-pity to " go out and do something kind to someone or other ".

That in itself often blesses the one who helps just as much as the one who is helped.

THE FRIENDSHIP BOOK

WHOSOEVER heareth these sayings of mine, and doeth them, I will liken him unto a wise man, which built his house upon a rock.

St Matthew 7, 24.

COUNT your garden by the flowers,
Never by the leaves that fall.
Count your day by golden hours,
Don't remember clouds at all.

Count your nights by stars, not shadows,
Count your life by smiles, not tears,
And, with joy on every birthday,
Count your age by friends — not years.

ARTUR RUBENSTEIN, the famous pianist, lived to be 95 years old and he was still performing in public when he was 90. One had only to watch him playing to realise the enormous joy he got out of his work.

Someone once asked him about the secret of his exuberance. How could he play so enthusiastically pieces which he must have played so many hundreds of times before?

He replied, " I try to imagine I am playing each piece for the very first time so the music comes new to me every time."

I can't help thinking that is a principle we could apply to very many aspects of our lives. What a lot of boredom it would save us when we are doing what we call " the daily round, the trivial task ".

OH what a happy soul am I!
Although I cannot see,
I am resolved that in this world
Contented I will be.

No-one would pretend that verse has much literary merit, but when we remember that it was written by a little blind girl only eight years old it takes on a new value.

That small girl, Fanny Crosby, went on to be one of the world's most prolific hymn writers, many of whose compositions were used in the Moody and Sankey Revival. Some put the number of her hymns as high as 7000 of which now probably only " Rescue the perishing " and " Safe in the arms of Jesus " are remembered.

She lived to be 92 and in addition to her hymn-writing she was a teacher in a blind institute, a speaker and a prison visitor. She more than fulfilled the determination she expressed in her childhood verse.

MANY writers on prayer have been at pains to point out that one of its most important functions is not to persuade God to do something we want Him to do for us, but to put ourselves in the position where we know what it is that God wants us to do.

However, the truth can scarcely ever have been put more tellingly than in the words of the 18th century Biblical commentator, Matthew Henry: " When a boatman puts out his boathook and fastens it to the shore, it is not to draw the shore to his boat, but to draw his boat to the shore."

THE FRIENDSHIP BOOK

ON one of her lecture trips to South Africa, Winifred Holtby, author of the famous novel, " South Riding ", had a particularly depressing and upsetting time. This was followed, however, by a peaceful train journey among the mountains with their flowering aloes and yellow mimosa, while beyond was the blue sea and white dazzling sands.

She writes about this experience: " Oh, eyes are happy things—all that they see. It is surprising that they keep company for three score years and ten with our unquiet minds."

" Eyes are happy things "—a quaint phrase perhaps, yet how often, like Winifred Holtby, we can find relief from the pressures of life as our eyes drink in happily the beauty that is all around us, the wonders of earth and sea and sky.

DO you like tongue-twisters, Mr Gay?" asked young Billy when I was talking to him the other day.

" No, I can't say I do, Billy," I replied.

" Neither do I," he grinned, and then recited a verse which apparently had been going the rounds at his school:

> *I never like tongue-twisters,*
> *They make my ire erupt;*
> *Every time I try one*
> *My tang gets tongueled up!*

I WAITED patiently for the Lord; and he inclined unto me, and heard my cry.   Psalm 40, 1.

THE FRIENDSHIP BOOK

LORD NUFFIELD is noteworthy for the vast sums of money he contributed to worthy causes. He is said to have given away over £30 million during his lifetime. His example still lives on.

In Oxford, which owes much of its prosperity to Lord Nuffield and the range of Morris cars, lived a stonemason and his wife. Mr and Mrs John Snow had no children, so they gave their life savings, amounting to several thousand pounds, to hospitals in the Oxford area. They admitted that what they did was directly due to the example set by Lord Nuffield himself.

A PREACHER friend once said to me that if from a sermon any member of the congregation goes away with just one good thought the preacher should be well pleased.

I did come away from church the other Sunday with one such thought and I am sure it will stay with me for a long time. The preacher was talking about the incident where Jesus and his disciples were caught in a storm on the Sea of Galilee. He said that most of us probably feel that the most dramatic moment in that story is when the wind abated and the waves subsided and all was quiet: peace after the storm.

But he went on to say that he thought that the really dramatic moment was earlier in the story when Jesus lay quietly and peacefully asleep in the stern of the boat while the storm raged. That was peace *in* the storm—not *after* the storm.

I confess I had never quite seen the story like that, but isn't this what faith is all about—that we may have peace *amid* the storms of life?

THE FRIENDSHIP BOOK

IN old age, Goya, the 18th-century Spanish artist had such bad eyesight that others had to sharpen his pencils for him, but this did not prevent him doing some marvellous drawings up to almost the end of his life.

One of his last drawings is of a bearded, bent old man, supporting himself upon two sticks. Its title is " Aun Aprendo " which means, " I am still learning ".

Who could really grow old with a philosophy like that?

A LITTLE girl sat scribbling. " Oh, Sarah's always writing little stories," her family used to say. Her father kept a bookshop so Sarah Smith had plenty to read, too.

Even when she was older, Sarah never thought of submitting any of her stories for publication. It was her sister who sent one of her tales to Charles Dickens, at that time editing a magazine.

To Sarah's amazement, Dickens wrote accepting her story and paid her £5 for it. He also asked for more!

That was the beginning of a career in writing. In 1866 " Jessica's First Prayer " was published in a magazine called " Sunday at Home ". Lord Shaftesbury liked it and wrote to her under her pseudonym of Hesba Stretton. The story became a bestseller and Hesba Stretton a famous writer.

She was deeply concerned about the cruelty and neglect of children and became one of the founders of the Society for the Prevention of Cruelty to Children.

Today one can see a memorial window dedicated to her, in the church at Church Stretton, Shropshire.

COOL WATERS

THE FRIENDSHIP BOOK

EDNA MASON of Sutton Coldfield has two friends in San Diego, USA, Professor and Mrs Conrad. Some time ago Professor Conrad sent Edna these verses which she forwarded to me. I am delighted to publish them:

Of the three greatest blessings
That come from above,
One is LIFE, one is HEALTH,
And the third one is LOVE.

May you take joy in LIFE,
Give your HEALTH the best care,
And send out your LOVE
To mankind everywhere.

I HEARD a story once of a man who went on a journey in search of happiness. He sought his goal for many years without success. At last, weary and in despair, he returned home and sat down outside it. He could see children playing on the village green and hear their joyful voices. The sun shone down on him and the world all around filled him with happiness. He could not believe it. He had discovered happiness where he least sought it.

He had learned that happiness is like a butterfly. Pursued, it is always beyond your grasp, but sometimes, if you sit quietly, it will come unexpectedly and alight upon you.

PRESERVE me, O God: for in thee do I put my trust.
                                             Psalm 16, 1.

THE FRIENDSHIP BOOK

A FRIEND tells me how proud his grandmother was of her garden but adds that she grew flowers not only for her own delight, but so she could give masses of them to other people. She used to say, " I give my flowers as bouquets, not as wreaths!"

I am sure she would have approved of some words written by one Berton Braley:

If with pleasure you are viewing any work a man is doing,

If you like him or you love him, tell him now.

Do not wait till life is over and he's underneath the clover,

For he cannot read his tombstone when he's dead!

I MEANT to say it, but didn't like to."

" I ought to have said it, but somehow I didn't seem to get the right opportunity."

" I wish I'd said how grateful I was, but . . ."

How often such comments are heard! How often have you thought or said something similar? Personally I've often been remiss in saying a word of kindness perhaps because I was in a hurry.

And what about encouragement? Perhaps the tea-cosy knitted by little Jenny is lumpy in the wrong places, but instead of noticing this, why not praise the neat stitches or the chosen colour? There is always something that can be praised.

Then gratitude—do we always express our genuine gratitude as we really feel it, or do we merely murmur " thank you"?

The strange thing is that the more outgoing we are at expressing our genuine feelings, the more other people respond!

GOLDEN DAYS

Though all too brief our holidays,
When humdrum life resumes once more,
They leave us hosts of memories
To treasure in our private store.

WEDNESDAY—AUGUST 20.

I HAVE been pondering all week a striking thought which came to me from our minister's sermon last Sunday: " If you divide material treasure among a thousand people, each person has a thousandth part; but if you divide spiritual treasure among a thousand people each has the whole."

It's true of so many things, isn't it? Because I enjoy the sunshine, or a good book, or great music there isn't any less for you to enjoy! There is so much of which we can say, " It's *all* for me . . . and it's *all* for you!"

THURSDAY—AUGUST 21.

BEFORE their re-organisation into the one administrative region of Cumbria, there existed a friendly rivalry between the two counties of Cumberland and Westmorland. The Cumbrian would say, " There's nobbut two counties in England. And the second is Westmorland." The Westmorland retort was, " There's nobbut one county in England. And the folk frae Cumberland live next door."

And, as long as it is as friendly as that, why shouldn't we think our own place best?

FRIDAY—AUGUST 22.

WE couldn't get along without material possessions, but all the same it is important to see them in perspective. That's why I like these lines which I saw years ago on a calendar:

Wealth is not gold nor land, nor stately homes nor marts;
The only gold worth having is found in human hearts.

THE FRIENDSHIP BOOK

THERE is an old Indian story of a woman suffering from inconsolable grief who went to a holy man for help. He thought for some time and then said, "Take this bowl and visit every house in the city. From each home where sorrow has not entered, beg one grain of rice. When your bowl is full your grief will have disappeared."

Months later she visited him again. Her bowl was still empty, but on her face was a look of serenity.

"I could find no home where sorrow had not entered," she said. "But as my heart went out in sympathy to others, so the pain went from it."

O GIVE thanks unto the Lord; for he is good; for his mercy endureth for ever.   I Chronicles 16, 34.

WE have all heard of the horrors of the concentration camp at Ravensbruck during the Second World War. After it had been captured by the Allies, a piece of torn wrapping-paper was found on which an unknown prisoner had scribbled these lines:

"O Lord, remember not only the men and women of goodwill, but also those of illwill. But do not remember all the suffering they have inflicted on us; remember the fruits we have bought, thanks to this suffering—our comradeship, our loyalty, our humility, our courage, our generosity, the greatness of heart which has grown out of all this, and when they come to judgment, let all the fruits which we have borne be their forgiveness."

THE FRIENDSHIP BOOK

I WONDER if you've heard the legend of St Bega, the Irish princess who landed on the Cumberland coast asking if she could build an abbey. Lord Egremont cynically promised her she could have as much land as the snow would cover on Midsummer's Day. He thought he was pretty safe in basing his promise on such an unlikely event.

But the weather in the Lake District is notoriously unpredictable and it *did* snow on Midsummer's Day. Thus a fine abbey was built and its ruins can still be seen at St Bees, which is named after St Bega.

It's easy to admire Bega, the saint who founded the Abbey, but Lord Egremont comes out of the story well, too. He didn't expect to lose the bargain, but when he did, he kept his word.

SEEDTIME and harvest, cold and heat, Summer and Winter, day and night "—so the Biblical writer reminds us of the rhythm that runs through the whole of life.

A mother singing lullabies to her baby; little children chanting nursery rhymes or skipping and dancing; soldiers marching; drums beating; waves lapping on the shore; birds' wings flapping as they fly—life is full of rhythm.

I am sure that as we *notice* these rhythms and share in them—listening sometimes to our breathing or the beating of our heart, tapping our feet to music, putting some rhythm into our walking, we get a strange sense of being part of the rhythm of the whole of life.

Try it—it can be an exhilarating experience.

GARDEN BOUNTY

I SUPPOSE that for all of us there are people of whom we have said, " I don't like so-and-so." I am afraid I have said it myself sometimes, but I shall certainly try not to do so again after listening to a mother talking to her small boy in the park the other day.

" I don't like Tommy," he said.

" Why ever not?" asked Mother.

" He is always thumping people."

" Well, that's *not* nice," said Mother, " but it's only one part of Tommy. Why not try saying, ' I rather like Tommy, but I don't like him thumping people'?"

Lucky boy to have such a sensible and understanding mother!

SIR FRANCIS CROSSLEY, the 19th century Halifax philanthropist, was once on a tour of America when he was entranced with a magnificent sunset near Mount Washington. He wrote afterwards that as he stood there the following thought came to him: " It is true you cannot bring the many thousands you have left in your native country to see this beautiful scenery, but you can take something of this to them. It is possible so to arrange art and nature that they shall be within the walk of every working man in Halifax; that he shall go to take his stroll there after he has done his hard day's toil and be able to get home again without being tired."

The result was Crossley's gift of the People's Park to Halifax, one of the first towns to have such a park. It still provides leisure and beauty more than a century later.

THE FRIENDSHIP BOOK

A NUMBER of years ago a lady guide at Ripon Cathedral, Yorkshire, showed an elderly man around the beautiful building. He was very impressed and when he was leaving, she said: " Now when you return to your home town you will be able to tell all your friends that you have visited Ripon Cathedral."

The old man smiled: " But Ripon is my home town. I've lived here for over 80 years. It's the first time though, that I've ever ventured into the Cathedral. I wish I'd discovered it sooner."

How many folk are like that? Treasures lie on our doorsteps and even if we see scores of tourists going to visit them, we don't follow their example. I'm told that quite a lot of people living in and around Haworth have never been inside the Brontë Parsonage Museum!

It is a little like the legend of the Swaffham Pedlar. John Chapman, a 15th century pedlar, set out from his native Swaffham to seek his fortune in London. On arrival he met a man who told him that he had dreamed of a pot of gold in a Swaffham pedlar's garden. Back trudged John and his faithful dog and on digging in his garden, did indeed find the gold.

A place-name sign at Swaffham depicts John and his dog setting out for London together with the words: " Ye tinker of Swaffham who did by a dream find a great fortune."

W HILE the earth remaineth, seedtime and harvest, and cold and heat, and summer and winter, and day and night shall not cease.

Genesis 8, 22.

SEPTEMBER

MONDAY—SEPTEMBER 1.

ACCORDING to ancient legend, St Fiacre (whose festival day it is today) was an Irish prince who went to France in the 7th century and became a hermit.

His reputation for holiness was so great that crowds of pilgrims came to visit him. He felt bound to feed them when they came and so there in the wilderness, around his hermitage, he is said to have grown splendid herbs and vegetables although the conditions were so unpromising. It was through this that he came eventually to be adopted as the patron saint of gardeners.

TUESDAY—SEPTEMBER 2.

VERY many people, including the great and the gifted, stood in awe of the 18th century writer, Dr Samuel Johnson.

His scathing wit and his power to deflate the pompous, as well as his outstanding brilliance made him both respected and feared as he sat at dinner parties and in coffee houses with the society of his day.

But there was another side to Dr Johnson of which even many of his friends were unaware. Often the guests in his home were not the famous and accomplished, but the poor, the aged, the hungry, the blind and the needy of any sort. Out of his fairly slender means he was always ready to help others less fortunate than himself, a side of his character too often overlooked. And that is the Dr Johnson I like to remember.

QUIET CORNER

THE FRIENDSHIP BOOK

DURING the Battle of Britain in 1940, the Prime Minister visited the Headquarters of the Air Vice-Marshal who was commanding the vital No. 11 Group.

On the radar screen Winston Churchill watched the German bombers drawing nearer, and as each wave approached, the Air Vice-Marshal ordered the British fighter squadrons to repel them.

It seemed as if the waves of German bombers would never cease, and at last the Prime Minister asked: " How many more have you got?" Without any change of inflexion in his voice, the Air Vice-Marshal said: " I'm putting in my last."

The two men gazed at the screen, waiting for the next wave of enemy bombers. They never came. There had been just enough British fighter squadrons to put into the air against the enemy.

With tears in his eyes, Winston Churchill got into his car, and on the way back to London he composed the immortal words: " Never, in the field of human conflict, has so much been owed by so many to so few."

Surely one of the most moving stories of the War.

OF course we all want to be liked. It's the most natural thing in the world. Sometimes, though, it is necessary to be unpopular if we are to stick to our principles, keep our integrity and have a clear conscience.

The writer G. K. Chesterton found that his principles often got him into trouble, but he used to say, " I like getting into hot water. It keeps me clean!"

K

THE FRIENDSHIP BOOK

MRS DAWSON is 85. She lives on her own in a roomy flat and manages to cope very well, with a little assistance from her home help and friendly neighbours.

"I know how important it is to turn up at the funeral of a relation or friend," she was telling me the other day. "But, you see, because I can't travel very far I have had to miss many funerals I would like to have gone to. But do you know what I do instead?"

Then she told me how, at the hour when the funeral is taking place, she always goes to the church near her home and spends a short while in silent prayer, thinking of the one who has died and those left behind.

Thus, in her own quiet way she pays tribute just as sincerely as those attending the funeral.

VISITORS to the home of a successful business-man were surprised to notice that though most of the house was beautifully and expensively furnished, one room had old, very shabby, furnishings.

At last one of his friends asked him about it. His answer was, "I came from very humble beginnings. That old furniture was the first we ever had and most of it was bought second-hand. The rest of the house reminds me just where I have *arrived,* but that room reminds me where I've come *from!*"

A bit romantic? Even sentimental? Maybe. Yet there is much in the past of most of us, which, if we remembered it humbly and gratefully, might make us better people.

THE FRIENDSHIP BOOK

THE Lord called Samuel: and he answered, Here am I.

I Samuel 3, 4.

WHEN we think of saints we sometimes have a vision of someone with their head in the clouds, not very much concerned with the bread-and-butter things of life.

That picture is often very far from the truth. One of the best-loved saints, St Teresa, ran her convents with great efficiency and once told a group of novices: " We don't want any more saints here. What we want are some good scrubbers."

St Teresa would have approved, I am sure, of her modern namesake, Mother Teresa, whose work among the sick and destitute of Calcutta shows how love and compassion can be channelled into tireless practical help for those in need.

THE harvest hymn, " To Thee, O Lord, our hearts we raise ", the Christmas hymn, " As with gladness men of old ", and " Come unto me, ye weary ", were all written last century by William Chatterton Dix, an insurance official. What is more, they were all done at different periods in Dix's life when he was ill in bed, or recovering from illness.

He himself remarked on the curious fact that " most of my best-known hymns were written when I was suffering from some bodily ailment." But is it really so curious? Is it not just one more example of the way in which mind and spirit triumph over physical weakness?

WELL DONE

THE FRIENDSHIP BOOK

I LOVE stories which tell of the human side of great men and women.

Years ago, on a winter's night, the dining room of a large house in North America was brilliantly lighted, and the table set for a meal. All the guests were ready except one. A servant said that he had arrived an hour before and been shown to a room where he could wash and rest before dinner. At last the host excused himself and went upstairs to find the missing guest.

On his way he had to pass the nursery, and there was the man, a baby astride his foot. He was " riding the child to Boston ", and singing lustily, to the delight of another small child standing by. When he saw his host, he finished the song and then rose to bid the children goodnight.

The father said to the children, " Say ' Goodnight, and thank you, General George Washington.' "

And so they called " Goodnight " to a great man — a man humble enough to forget his dinner and his fellow-guests in order to sing and play with the children.

D ID you hear about the two neighbouring seaside resorts which were in fierce competition with each other to attract visitors?

One of them hit on the idea of hiring out wind-breaks—canvas sheets mounted on poles—for visitors to erect on the sands. The next year their rivals, not to be out-done, followed suit—but with a difference. They called theirs " sun-traps"!

Clever publicity that, but, when you come to think about it, not a bad philosophy of life, too!

THE FRIENDSHIP BOOK

A FRIEND occasionally sends me the order of service leaflet of the church she attends. Members of the congregation are invited to place a " thought for the week " in a box in the vestibule and the minister selects one or more with which to head the service paper, sometimes using it as the theme of the service.

A recent " thought " was: " Write your injuries in dust, your benefits in marble."

You may not be surprised to know that one of the hymns sung that day was, " Count your many blessings, name them one by one ".

I LIKE people who are big enough to tell stories against themselves. One of the most amusing examples I know is that of a Carmelite monk who was comparing other monastic orders with his own.

" Of course," he said, " I know that as far as scholarship is concerned we cannot compare with the Benedictines, and when it comes to charity and good works the Franciscans beat us hollow, but as far as humility is concerned we are superior to everyone upon earth!"

I am sure he had his tongue in his cheek when he said that, but it underlines the difficulty of true humility — the danger of being proud of being humble!

I forget who it was who wrote:
Humble must he be who to heaven would go,
High is the roof there, but the door is low.

In a world where there is so much arrogance and self-assertion, the need for humility and self-forgetfulness is even more vital.

THE FRIENDSHIP BOOK

WHOSOEVER shall give you a cup of water to drink in my name, because ye belong to Christ, verily I say unto you, he shall not lose his reward.

St Mark 9, 41.

I KNOW a minister who asked a firm to do a poster for his church notice-board with the heading: " HARVEST THANKSGIVING SERVICE."

The sign-writer looked a little doubtful and then said, " Would it be all right if I put HARVEST FESTIVAL instead?"

" But why?" asked the minister.

" Well," was the reply, " there really isn't room on the board for ' Thanksgiving '."

There should always be room on the board—and in our hearts—for that.

DURING a holiday in North Wales, the Lady of the House and I spent a few hours in the ancient city of Bangor. Adjoining the Cathedral is a Bible Garden containing flowers, plants and trees mentioned in the Bible accompanied by appropriate Biblical references and texts. Among them, of course, was the familiar, " Consider the lilies . . ."

I couldn't help thinking that when we look at flowers our reaction is, " How lovely they are . . ." or " How sweetly they smell . . ." But it wasn't either of these things which Jesus mentioned. He said, " Consider the lilies, how they *grow*." This was the real miracle of the flowers—not just their beauty or their fragrance, but their *growth*, their *life*.

THE FRIENDSHIP BOOK

ONE of the greatly-honoured names in the Salvation Army in India during the early part of this century was Booth-Tucker. He spent many years as an itinerant preacher going from village to village and helping in any way he could.

Unhappily, his efforts were not always appreciated and he met with much indifference and even hostility. On one occasion he was even more badly treated than usual and had to flee for his life from a village where he had been preaching.

After several miles he fell asleep exhausted under a tree. When he woke up he was startled to find himself surrounded by natives. They were from the village which had driven him out, but instead of the hostile treatment he had encountered there, he found them looking down at him with friendliness and compassion.

He discovered that they had followed him from the village intending to kill him, but as he lay there asleep, they saw his feet and noticed for the first time that he walked barefoot as they did. In some strange way this marked him out as one of themselves. Carefully they carried him back to the village and attended to him, and this time readily listened to what he had to say.

" He's one of us." " She's one of us." What a bond this can be with all kinds of people.

A VICAR met one of his flock in the street and said to him, " I didn't see you in church on Sunday — In fact, I hear you were playing golf instead."

Came the honest reply: " That's not true, Vicar — and I've got the fish to prove it!"

THE FRIENDSHIP BOOK

A FRIEND who recently returned from a holiday in Turkey where he visited a Turkish carpet factory discovered an unusual thing about these beautiful pieces of craftsmanship. Through years of use the millions of knots in a carpet tighten, giving the carpet an increasingly hard-wearing quality and beauty, so that, in fact, an old, used Turkish carpet is more valuable than a new one.

A thought perhaps for those of us for whom the years seem to be passing all too quickly—there *are* blessings and rewards in growing old. It can be a good and pleasant time if we are prepared to see it as such.

L ITTLE Michelle Rodgers of Falmouth was only eight years old when her class at school was asked to write a short essay saying what they understood by the word " peace "—a pretty formidable task, you might think for children so young.

But Michelle was equal to the challenge as you will see, for this is what she wrote:

" What is peace? Peace is something quiet, not a noise, not a quarrel. Peace is very nice. It's something calm. No war, no fights. People who murder — that isn't peace. Peace is love, peace is gentle, peace is not rough. Peace is when people meet and make friends, peace is doing something quiet. Peace is not killing, peace is playing. We should let animals have peace and freedom, we should let Nature have space and room to grow. Peace was when Jesus was born. Peace is happiness. Peace is when children play and make new friends. Peace is wonderful."

Well said, Michelle.

YEAR ROUND

The patient horse, the toiling men
Have given way to new machines,
But still the farmer must observe
The same old seasonal routines.

THE FRIENDSHIP BOOK

O LORD our Lord, how excellent is thy name in all the earth!   Psalm 8, 9.

IT is not long since size seemed to be the measure of worth . . . big was beautiful! Now, with the advent of micro-chip technology, things have gone in the other direction. Even our small neighbour, Billy, is up to the minute in this respect:

"Mr Gay, did you hear of the man who went into the micro-chip business in town? He's very successful."

"Is he?" I said, impressed.

"Yes," said Billy as he ran off. "He's already moving into smaller premises!"

SOME years ago, the artist Norman Wilkinson drew a series of sketches of English cathedrals for a magazine. A few years later, he did similar drawings of English castles.

About the latter he wrote, "As I sketched these castles I contrasted them with the cathedrals I had previously drawn. With few exceptions the castles were lifeless ruins, the pageantry all gone. But the cathedrals, with glorious stained glass and carving all in perfect order, were living things which even war-time bombing had left almost untouched. Cathedrals of religion stand intact, while many of the castles, built for war, are in ruins."

A vivid reminder to us all of the importance of living and working, in our own quiet way, for the things of truth and beauty and love and peace.

THE FRIENDSHIP BOOK

HENRY WARD BEECHER, the famous American preacher, used to tell the story of an unemployed stonemason who went to Brooklyn in search of work. Finding a large building in course of construction, he approached the foreman and asked him for work. The foreman gave him a small piece of a large design and told him to carve it in stone.

When he had completed the work, he took it to the foreman who gave him another similar task. This went on for some time and the mason felt a little disappointed that he wasn't given something bigger to do, but he carried on putting all his skill and effort into these small pieces.

When at last the building was completed and the scaffolding removed, showing the building in all its splendour, the mason was astonished to find that all his small pieces of work, which at the time he did them seemed so insignificant, had been fitted together to make one of the outstanding features of the front of the building.

Overcome with emotion he cried, " I'm glad I did it well! I'm glad I did it well!"

Like that mason, we may often think the small deeds we do don't matter very much. This story shows, I think, how wrong we can be.

A CERTAIN Scottish peer prided himself on his fitness, even when he was old. One day in church, a visiting clergyman referred to him in prayer as " Thine aged and infirm servant ".

Highly indignant, the old man insisted on taking the minister on a 25-mile tramp over the hills and ended up by carrying him home on his back!

THE FRIENDSHIP BOOK

IN her book " In Pleasant Places," the popular entertainer, the late Joyce Grenfell, tells of her visits to Australia and of the many friends she made there. One introduced her to another and so the circle grew.

This gave rise to a happy thought. We make out our Family Trees, she said, but how exciting to make " A Friendship Tree " with its spreading branches.

Why not try it? You may be surprised to find just how many friends you have.

A BEAUTIFUL old legend tells of a cooper — a barrel-maker — who was notorious for his meanness and greed. One day an old man, dressed in rags, stood at the door of the cooper's workshop and asked for a drink of water.

" Go to the well in the village if you want water," snarled the cooper. " I never give to beggars." He expected the beggar to shuffle away, but instead, to his astonishment, the old man drew himself to his full height and in ringing tones cried, " Cooper! You shall be punished for your meanness. Take a barrel to the well and fill it with water."

As the cooper hesitated, his visitor added in tones that could not be disobeyed, " Now!" The cooper rolled his barrel to the well, but though he sank it in the water it refused to fill. Time and time again he tried to no avail, and at last he realised that this was the punishment his strange visitor had prophesied. This was the consequence of his meanness.

He began to shed tears of sorrow and penitence. One of his tears fell into the barrel, which suddenly filled to the brim and overflowed. He was forgiven.

THE FRIENDSHIP BOOK

IN six days the Lord made heaven and earth, the sea, and all that in them is, and rested the seventh day: wherefore the Lord blessed the sabbath day, and hallowed it. Exodus 20, 11.

GEORGE BERNARD SHAW—the bank clerk who became a world-famous playwright — achieved his success by patience and relentless determination. He set himself the plan of writing five pages a day, allowing no circumstance to interfere with that aim. The first nine years were heart-breaking. He reckoned that in those years his earnings worked out at about a penny a day!

A lesser man would have given up. He kept on—and achieved international respect. There's no substitute for hard work, is there?

RECENTLY, when I was calling on an elderly friend, she surprised me by asking for my autograph. Politely I did my best to hide my surprise, but then she laughed. "Here is my 'autograph book,'" she said, and produced a large patchwork quilt. Nearly every patch contained a signature, each one beautifully embroidered over in fine stitches. I read the names, wondering if there were any well known ones among them, but she explained, "You won't find any public figures there. I only collect the signatures of my special friends—they are of far more value to me."

I gladly wrote my signature on one of the empty patches.

OCTOBER

WEDNESDAY—OCTOBER 1.

ON 1st October 1885, the people of Britain mourned the death of Lord Shaftesbury, the philanthropist who had battled for many good causes. The one best remembered nowadays was his campaign to prevent small children being employed in factories and mines and as little climbing boys for chimney sweeps.

It has been said that his remarkable insight into how utterly wretched a child can be was partly due to his own unhappy childhood and his experiences at his first school in Chiswick. In later life he always spoke of the family servant, Maria Millis, as his great friend and she was certainly responsible in fostering his Christian outlook on life.

Nor were circumstances always easy for him in adult life. Often he was very short of money, yet it never stopped him from helping other people. When he inherited the family estate at Wimborne, St Giles, Dorset, he discovered it had been sadly neglected. The cottage dwellings were dreadful. He set about selling land and family pictures in order to rehouse his tenants.

No, things were not easy for Anthony Ashley Cooper, Lord Shaftesbury, who, when he died, left the world a better place.

THURSDAY—OCTOBER 2.

MY heart goes out to the small boy who, asked what he wanted for his birthday, answered without a moment's hesitation, "I want to stop having piano lessons!"

THE FRIENDSHIP BOOK

IN a book on bird life I was interested to read the author's comment that shore birds and gulls face into the wind when they are at rest on the beach, thus keeping their feathers unruffled.

A parable from Nature indeed, for, when you think about it, it is people who *face* their troubles who manage to remain unruffled!

TODAY is the feast day of St Francis of Assisi who, in the 12th century, relinquished the wealth and amusements of a " young man about town " for the life of a travelling friar.

Once, he and a fellow friar sat down on a stone near a fountain to eat the bread they had begged in the town. Francis is quoted as saying, " Not only are we filled with plenty but our treasure is of God's own providing; for consider this bread which has come to us like manna, and this table of stone fit for the feasting of kings, and this well of bright water which is beverage from heaven."

Few can follow St Francis's austerity, nor did he expect or encourage people to do so. Most of them, he realised, must carry on the work of the world.

But wouldn't we all be happier if the notes of simplicity and great thankfulness which that story shows were the marks of our life, too?

GIVE unto the Lord the glory due unto his name: bring an offering, and come before him: worship the Lord in the beauty of holiness.

I Chronicles 16, 29.

THE FRIENDSHIP BOOK

I WONDER if you know Rudyard Kipling's story " The Ship that found Herself "? The cargo steamer *Dimbula* had been launched, and the owner's daughter who had performed the ceremony was talking to the captain.

" Now she's a real ship, isn't she?" the girl said delightedly.

" Oh, she's no' so bad," said the Scots captain cautiously. " But it takes more than christenin' to make a ship . . . she's just iron and rivets and plates put into the form of a ship. She has to find herself yet. She's all here, but the parts have not learned to work together yet."

The story goes on to tell of her maiden voyage and a great storm at sea. At the end of it, as she sailed into New York, " Her funnel was dirty grey from top to bottom; two boats had been carried away; three copper ventilators looked like hats after a fight . . . the bridge had a dimple in the middle of it."

But the ship was a real ship now, not just rivets, iron and plates. She had " found herself ". I don't know whether Rudyard Kipling meant this to be a parable of life — living and working together in storm and stress and " finding ourselves " — but it *is* that, isn't it?

E LLEN THORNEYCROFT FOWLER is perhaps best known for the harvest hymn " Now the year is crowned with blessing ". She once made this perceptive comment: " It is better to build a cathedral than to make a boot; but I think it is better actually to make a boot than only to dream about building a cathedral."

L

THE FRIENDSHIP BOOK

A MISCHIEVOUS boy was asked by his mother: "How do you expect to get into heaven?"

He thought a minute and then said: "Well, I'll just run in and out and keep slamming the door until they say: 'For goodness sake, come in or stay out!' and then I'll go in."

I SUPPOSE that one of the most popular and long-lived tunes is the "Londonderry Air", which has been described as "one of the most beautiful folk songs in the world". It is so old that no-one knows when it was written or who composed it. It was handed down from generation to generation, not in printed form but by the human voice, probably being adapted and altered until it reached the near-perfection of the tune we know and love now.

The words "Danny Boy" are often sung to this tune and I have a record of this which I must have played many hundreds of times, always with enjoyment, but never so much as after I read some words of the music critic, James Dudley, which helped me to understand it better.

He wrote, "Notice how it begins calmly and rather sadly, how it slowly and gradually works up higher and higher until it reaches a note of triumph, then subsides again and ends on a note of calm."

Next time you hear this wonderful tune, try to follow it with that description in mind. I am sure it will mean even more to you than before. Not only that, I am sure it will lead you to feel of so many things, as I do, that the more we *know* of anything — be it music, a picture, an old cathedral, or a wayside flower, the more fully we can enjoy it.

THE FRIENDSHIP BOOK

ONE friendly face in a crowd of strangers — how it makes your day! Someone with a smile of kindness and a pleasant way; park bench becomes inducement to friendly armchair chat, it breaks through a shell of loneliness to talk of this and that. You may not ever meet again but still it warms the heart, two strangers close-knit for a while, instead of worlds apart; such brief encounters leave behind a haunting, sweet perfume, remembered like the muted strain of an old familiar tune.

THE year is getting on," my grandmother used to say as we entered October, which made it seem as if Winter was just round the corner! It isn't really.

Indeed, this time of the year can often bring balmy, pleasant days—an Indian Summer, we sometimes call it. The expression seems to have come from North America where there is often a period of warm, calm, dry weather which gave the American Indian farmers an extended period to prepare for the Winter.

In some country districts in England, the term " St. Luke's Summer " was used, since that saint's feast day fell in the midst of this often delightful spell of weather.

Whatever we call it, let us rejoice in, and use to full advantage, the good days left to us before Winter closes in.

WITH God all things are possible.

St Matthew 19, 26.

JUST LOOK . . .

Colours bright and colours gay,
And what a picture's here to stay!

THE FRIENDSHIP BOOK

WHEN Mozart was only four he was asked how he composed music. He answered, " I just put together little notes that like each other."

That's why friends are so important. Together we can make life quite a symphony!

LOOKING through some old magazines recently, I came across photographs of people on holiday at the seaside at the beginning of this century — the ladies in broad-brimmed hats and voluminous skirts, the men in thick serge suits and bowler hats. What a job they must have had packing for a holiday in those days!

Looking at those pictures reminded me of a passage in a book called " My First Eighty Years " by Helen Wilson. She wrote, " Has it ever struck you that handy little suitcases are a modern invention? Our grandparents travelled with chests, large or not so large, or with cardboard boxes unashamed. Remember the old lady who, anxious to lose none of her things, kept repeating the inventory throughout the journey, ' Big box, little box, hand-box, bundle '?"

How different was the case of two young people who stayed the weekend with the Lady of the House and me recently. All their possessions were packed in one small rucksack which they took turns in carrying on their journey.

Much as we may appreciate many of the amenities of modern existence, I am sure there is a moral for us somewhere there about the enjoyment we can find, at least some of the time, from a simple, uncluttered life.

WEDNESDAY—OCTOBER 15.

I RENE BERNAERTS wrote this lovely prayer in verse on behalf of all parents of young children:

Within this room our children sleep,
Look down, dear Lord, we pray,
And may Your angels vigil keep
Until the break of day.
Send down a benediction, Lord,
Upon each sleeping head,
Help us to guide their ways aright
To follow where You led.
Within this room our children sleep,
We ask, dear Lord above,
That You will hear our prayer and bless
The children that we love.

THURSDAY—OCTOBER 16.

Y EARS ago, a friend of ours on holiday in Belgium made a special point of visiting the old town of Bruges in order to see the Memling Art Gallery of which he had heard so much.

He knew that it was somewhere near the church of Notre Dame, but he wandered up and down the narrow streets for some time without success. Finally, he stopped a passer-by to ask instructions.

" There it is," said the native of the town, pointing, " in the Hospital of St John."

In the hospital! That was the last place he would have thought of looking for the famous art collection. He expected it to be housed in some imposing building of its own; instead, it was in a comparatively small room, close to the hospital wards.

But isn't beauty often found in the most unexpected places? And isn't it all the more appreciated for that very reason?

THE FRIENDSHIP BOOK

THE sermon in church last Sunday was on a text I haven't heard preached on for years—" Who hath despised the day of small things?" from the prophecy of Zechariah. The preacher made the interesting point that in our world, what he called " Jumboism "—the vogue for sheer size in everything—was giving place to the age of the micro-chip, literally the day of small things!

I was reminded of a verse by Nora Gray:

For when God made the mountains,
He shaped the flowers as well,
And when he spread the ocean,
He formed the cockle-shell.
So do not be despising the day of little things,
For bees as well as angels can boast a pair of
wings.

With those lines and the sermon in my mind I came away from church feeling that even if some of the big things in life are beyond our power, we can exert a good deal of influence through the little ones.

A FRIEND of Robert Louis Stevenson once found him turning over the pages of a scrapbook containing cuttings of reviews of his own books.

" Well," she said jokingly, " Is fame all that it is cracked up to be?"

" Yes," said Stevenson quietly, " when I see my mother's eyes."

WHERE your treasure is, there will your heart be also.   St Matthew 6, 21.

THE FRIENDSHIP BOOK

THE nursery rhyme says that the king was in his counting house, counting out his money. We all count our money—or lack of it—at times, but there are many other riches worth counting as this poem seen in an old church magazine tells:

Count your joys instead of your woes,
Count your friends instead of your foes,
Count your courage instead of your fears,
Count your laughs instead of your tears,
Count your health instead of your wealth,
Count on God instead of yourself.

FROM time to time we have a visiting minister to our church who always brings a small blackboard on which he draws simple diagrams to illustrate his short address to the young people in the congregation.

Recently, he explained how, from the early days of the Church, the Greek letter X (Chi), being the initial letter of the name Christ, has been used as a symbol or reverent abbreviation of the name. Then, on his blackboard he showed how the letter X was composed of one letter V placed on top of an inverted letter V (Λ). The top V, he said, represented the love and power of God reaching down to us. The inverted V (Λ) at the bottom represents our reaching up to God.

I don't think any of us who saw that vivid illustration will ever forget it. It reminds me of some words spoken years ago by the then Archbishop of Canterbury, Dr William Temple: "Work as if everything depended upon you; pray as if everything depended upon God."

THE FRIENDSHIP BOOK

I SUPPOSE that nothing so reveals the real character of a man or a woman than the personal diaries they keep, for what is written there is usually meant for their eyes alone and is not intended for publication.

One such example is the diary of William Wilberforce, the anti-slavery campaigner. That campaign was carried out against what must have often been heart-breaking circumstances — the indifference of the vast majority of people, and fierce opposition from those with vested interests. A lesser man might have been tempted to give up the struggle. In addition to all this he had a great deal of personal trouble to bear.

Yet, in his diary, he doesn't dwell on this side of his life. A mere mention — and then it is dismissed. And on almost every page there are expressions of gratitude for blessings he had received from all kinds of people.

After one particularly poignant personal sorrow he writes: " No one has had such reason as myself to say that goodness and mercy have followed me all the days of my life."

How true it is that it is not so much what happens to us but how we react to it which is important.

THURSDAY—OCTOBER 23.

A TEACHER friend of ours says that the only time he tends to become impatient with his pupils is when one of them says of some subject or activity, " It's so boring!"

He tells them, " There is no such thing as a boring subject—only people who are bored!"

A very different thing indeed!

THE FRIENDSHIP BOOK

FRIDAY—OCTOBER 24.

THERE is an old saying, " Laugh and grow fat ";
certainly many modern medical authorities
believe that laughter can contribute to our health and
well-being. So did the writer of the biblical book of
Proverbs when he said, " A merry heart doeth good
like a medicine."

The 18th century writer John Wolcot (who wrote
under the nom-de-plume Peter Pindar) put the truth
even more dramatically:

Care to our coffin adds a nail, no doubt;
And every grin so merry draws one out.

Smile, please!

SATURDAY—OCTOBER 25.

MILLIONS of people must have heard of William
Carey, the pioneer missionary to India, but I
wonder how many people have heard of his sister
Mary who was bedridden and almost completely
paralysed for 50 years?

Carey used to tell what a great source of help and
inspiration Mary was to him amid the difficulty of his
mission. Great as the effort was, she struggled to
write him long letters about all that was of interest at
home, giving him encouragement and assuring him of
her constant prayers for his work. Her own minister,
Dr Gotch, used to say that " her work, in affliction,
was, in its way, as great as that of her brother ".

Truly a case of " the honoured—and the unsung ".

SUNDAY—OCTOBER 26.

TAKE therefore no thought for the morrow: for the
morrow shall take thought for the things of
itself. St Matthew 6, 34.

THE FRIENDSHIP BOOK

WHAT a lot we have still to learn from wise men of long ago. Lao Tse, whose name means " Grand Old Master ", was a Chinese sage who lived 600 years before the birth of Christ.

One of his famous sayings is, " To those who are good to me, let me be good. To those who are not good to me, let me also be good. Thus shall goodness be increased."

THE Lady of the House and I once took a short holiday in France and because our time was limited we took the quick way across the Channel, by hovercraft. It was a new experience for us — travelling, not on the surface of the water, but on a cushion of air.

Thousands of such crossings are now made every year, but when Christopher Cockerell demonstrated his invention in 1959 it was a tremendous breakthrough.

This is just one of the many examples of the way in which our lives have been enriched by the skill — and, not less, the imagination — of our inventors.

One of Cockerell's first experiments towards the fulfilment of his dream was to place a small tin inside a larger one and then to blow a jet of air into the space between them. Of course, that was only a beginning; many problems had to be overcome before the principle could be incorporated in the craft which carried the Lady of the House and me over a roughish sea in perfect comfort, in half an hour.

And to think, it all began with a couple of tin cans. An invention? Surely, like so much of life, almost a miracle!

WEDNESDAY—OCTOBER 29.

THESE lines were sent to me by Marion V. Stevenson of Victoria, British Columbia, Canada.

CONSCIENCE

Those who care
Are most aware
Of those who don't.

Those who don't
Are not aware
Of those who do.

Which one are you?

THURSDAY—OCTOBER 30.

I LIKE the story which Arthur Marshall, writer, broadcaster and ex-schoolmaster, tells of a geography teacher trying to be as kind as he could to one of his less bright pupils.

He wrote on his report, " He does well to find his way home."!

FRIDAY—OCTOBER 31.

A BUSINESS friend of ours who always seems to be caught up in a constant round of activities and good causes of one sort and another, was once asked whether he found any time for hobbies amid his busy life.

" Oh, yes," he said, " I have a great hobby — meeting people, talking to them, and finding out the best about them."

An admirable hobby indeed, and one that brings deep happiness.

NOVEMBER

SATURDAY—NOVEMBER 1.

VISITORS to lovely Grange-over-Sands in the Morecambe Bay area often climb to the top of Hampsfell. From here, 750 feet above sea level, there is a magnificent view of Morecambe, Heysham and Fleetwood to the south; the Lakeland mountains of Coniston Old Man, the Langdales and even Helvellyn to the west and the Pennines to the east.

At the top is a square building with a fenced round flat roof on which is a mountain indicator for visitors to trace their exact location.

This hospice was erected by the Rev. Thomas Remington as a shelter for wanderers on the fell in the last century and is still used today. Inside on its walls are the following verses, dated June, 1834:

A lengthen'd chain holds the door around,
To keep the cattle from the ground;
Kind reader: freely take your pleasure
But do no mischief to my treasure.

This Hospice has an open door,
Alike to welcome rich and poor,
A roomy seat for young and old
Where they may screen them from the cold.

Someone in May 1864 added a reply which ends,

Your offer made in kindly spirit
I hope you'll find our conduct merit.

SUNDAY—NOVEMBER 2.

VERILY I say unto you, No prophet is accepted in his own country. St Luke 4, 24.

THE FRIENDSHIP BOOK

THE other day on the radio I caught the closing lines of a song when I switched on for another programme. I don't know who the singer was and, as I say, it was just a snatch, but one, I think, worth remembering:

There is no such thing as time,
Only this very minute,
And I'm in it,
Thank the Lord.

OF all the thousands of people who every year admire the famous series of paintings by Michelangelo on the ceiling of the Sistine Chapel in Rome, I wonder how many realise that the artist was given this commission through the jealousy of a rival?

At the time, Michelangelo's fame was as a sculptor. A fellow-sculptor, jealous of his skill, persuaded the Pope to commission Michelangelo to paint the ceiling believing that, skilful though he was as a sculptor, he would not have the ability required as a painter and that failure would ruin his reputation and his career.

Instead, Michelangelo accepted the commission and worked at it for four years, ultimately achieving what has been described as " the mightiest series of paintings the world has ever seen."

Michelangelo knew all about his rival's jealousy but he did not allow this to affect him. He had a job to do and he got on with it, not troubling about what other people thought of him, but simply putting all he had into the task at hand.

Good advice for all of us — even though we may never become Michelangelos!

THE FRIENDSHIP BOOK

I LIKE the definition of repentance which says, "Repentance does not mean simply being sorry for what you have done, but being sorry enough to quit."

It ties up with the old story of someone burdened with a sense of wrong-doing who went to seek the help of a saintly old man whose reputation for wisdom was honoured far and wide.

"What must I do," he asked, "to be rid of this intolerable burden?"

"The answer is simple, my son," replied the old man. "You must repent, for God freely forgives those who are sorry for their wrong-doing and try sincerely to amend their lives."

"Yes, I know that," said the man. "What I do not know is *when* is the right time to repent."

"It is sufficient," was the reply, "if you repent the day before you die."

"The day before I die!" said the man in astonishment. "But how can I or anyone else possibly know that?"

"Exactly," said the wise old man. "So you must repent today lest you die tomorrow; and you must repent tomorrow lest you die the day after. So, you will live a life full of repentance and constantly receive the forgiveness of God."

B ISHOP WILLIAM STUBBS of Oxford once had a lengthy correspondence about whether a certain vicar should hang curtains behind the altar or not. In exasperation, the Bishop finally settled the matter with a note: "Dear Jones, Hang your curtains. Yours truly, W. Oxon."

THE SENTINEL

FRIDAY—NOVEMBER 7.

FEW books, I think, have as many quotable passages as those of Helen Keller, who, though blind, deaf, and, up to the age of ten, dumb, became a distinguished scholar, linguist and writer.

Here is one passage she wrote: " I have walked with people whose eyes are full of light, but who see nothing in wood, sea or sky, nothing in the city streets, nothing in books . . . It were far better to sail for ever in a night of blindness with sense and feeling and mind, than to be thus content with the mere act of seeing. They have the sunset, the morning skies, the purple of distant hills, yet their souls voyage through this enchanted world with a barren stare."

Do *we* truly *see?*

SATURDAY—NOVEMBER 8.

I HAVE been re-reading Charles Dickens's wonderful story *David Copperfield* and an incident struck me which I had never noticed before. It is when the spoiled, self-centred Steerforth (certainly not one of Dickens's most lovable characters) is bidding farewell to David. " Think of me at my best, old boy," were his parting words—and, in fact, they never met again.

It reminded me of the old verse,

There is so much good in the worst of us
And so much bad in the best of us,
That it hardly becomes any of us
To talk about the rest of us.

SUNDAY—NOVEMBER 9.

BLESSED are the peacemakers: for they shall be called the children of God.　　St Matthew 5, 9.

M

THE FRIENDSHIP BOOK

WHEN we called upon her the other day, our friend Mary was busy knitting squares to make blankets for some charitable cause.

" Do you enjoy knitting, Mary?" I asked.

She looked at me thoughtfully for a moment and then said, " I don't think I do really, Francis, but I do enjoy *this* because I know I am doing it for someone who *needs* it."

It reminds me of some words of J.B. Priestley who had been running a little competition in the village where he lived in which people were invited to write a short piece on " What Old People Need ". The things they mentioned were a room of their own, an occasional visitor, the means of sending an emergency message and so on. Priestley adds, " Several of them added that they needed to be needed. And surely it is too often forgotten that the old can give as well as take."

WHAT memorable and meaningful names John Bunyan invented for some of the places through which Christian passed in *The Pilgrim's Progress*—the Slough of Despond, Hill Difficulty, Doubting Castle, Vanity Fair.

One not so often recalled is Forgetful Green— " the most dangerous place in all these parts," Greatheart called it.

That *is* our danger, isn't it?—the danger of forgetting so much for which we ought to be grateful in so many ways, and at this Remembrancetide in particular, the sacrifices of those who suffered and died in war.

" Lest we forget."

THE FRIENDSHIP BOOK

THE ancient Chinese seem to have had a gift for putting a great deal of wisdom into very short sayings. One of their proverbs, which we might well ponder, says: " Be not disturbed at not being understood; be disturbed rather at not being understanding."

MANY readers who have holidayed in Staffordshire will probably have visited the estate of Alton Towers with its fascinating garden which includes an imitation Stonehenge, a decorative canal and a Chinese pagoda among its other features.

It becomes all the more impressive if one knows something about its origins. In 1814, John Talbot, 15th Earl of Shrewsbury, went to look at a piece of property he had inherited. There were the ruins of an old castle, an old house called Alton Lodge, and 600 acres of wilderness.

As he surveyed this unpromising scene, John Talbot saw in his mind's eye a glimpse of what it might become — a place of beauty with woodland, lakes, waterfalls, secluded paths, lofty towers peeping among the trees. For the remaining 13 years of his life, Talbot devoted the whole of his time and a large part of his fortune to making his dream come true.

In the grounds there is a statue in Talbot's memory bearing this inscription: " He made the desert smile." A wonderful epitaph. Few of us have the resources or the opportunities of John Talbot, but I can't help thinking that if we had the right kind of vision there is none of us who could not, through friendship and service and thoughtfulness, do something to make deserts smile!

SIR WILLIAM OSLER, the famous Canadian physician and professor of medicine, always had his lectures crowded with students eager to share his skill and knowledge.

But one of them, who later became a prominent physician, said that the greatest lesson he ever learned from Osler was from the opening words of one of his lectures: " Gentlemen," he said, " the first requisite in the care of a patient is to care!"

No wonder William Osler was a great doctor.

LAST Sunday evening in church we sang the hymn which includes the verse:

As o'er each continent and island,
The dawn leads on another day,
The voice of prayer is never silent,
Nor dies the strain of praise away.

It set me searching, when I came home, for some words which, long ago, I had copied down in one of my notebooks. I found them, but I have no note of who said them. This is what that unknown author wrote:

" Have you ever thought of Sunday going round the world? Where does it begin? Away in New Zealand and Fiji, 12 hours before it reaches us. In the meantime it crosses the Atlantic, goes across America and ends, 12 hours after leaving us, at Honolulu in the mid-Pacific . . . To join in Christian worship is to join overselves, not merely with a single congregation, but with a great number, out of every kindred and people and nation and tongue."

A good thought, I think, for those of us who look forward to sharing in Christian worship tomorrow!

THE FRIENDSHIP BOOK

LET not thy left hand know what thy right hand doeth.
St Matthew 6, 3.

DO you know this old poem?
Two brothers once lived down this way,
And one was Do, and one was Say.
If streets were dirty, taxes high,
Or schools were crowded, Say would cry:
" Oh, what a town!" But Brother Do
Would set to work to make things new.
And while Do worked, Say still would cry:
" He does it wrong! I know that I
Could do it right!" So all the day
Was heard the clack of Brother Say.
But this one fact from none was hid
—Say always talked, Do always did.

IN a television programme the poet John Betjeman and the artist John Piper were discussing their mutual love of churches. " Why is it, do you think," one asked the other, " that we both love churches so much?"

After just a moment's hesitation the answer came, " I suppose it's because they are always there . . . or have been for so long. They give a sense of stability amid so much that changes."

Haven't you felt like this sometimes about some of these ancient buildings? I know I have. But whether it is churches, or something else, happy are we if there is *something* that gives us a sense of stability.

THE FRIENDSHIP BOOK

THE telephone rang and five-year-old Jonathan answered it. It was his grandfather. After a little chat, Jonathan called out, " Mummy, come quickly—it's Grandpa. The one in London, not the one in Heaven!"

I WONDER if you know a book called " My Lady of the Chimney Corner "? It is probably out of print now for its author died over 40 years ago, but in its day the book must have influenced several generations of readers.

It was written by Alexander Irvine, an Irish preacher, lecturer and author, and is a tribute to his mother whom in the book he calls Anna. He tells how she lived most of her life in poverty and ill health in a tiny Irish cabin, seldom leaving her own fireside. This is why Irvine calls her " My Lady of the Chimney Corner "; but that chimney corner, as someone has said, " became a throne ".

In the little community where she lived, she was renowned for her willingness to listen patiently to all who came to her with their problems and for the wise counsel which she gave them.

Irvine was active and travelled widely yet he confessed that in many ways Anna's ministry was more effective than his own.

I never think of her without being reminded of the hymn which many of us used to sing in Sunday School days, " You in your small corner and I in mine." But was Anna's really a small corner? Was John Bunyan's prison cell a small corner? Our own " small corners" can, if we let them, be places of wide and loving influence.

FRIDAY—NOVEMBER 21.

E. V. LINDSAY, the author of " Losing Religion To Find It," also wrote these lines titled " The New Decalogue ":

Thou shalt not cling, thou shalt not clutch,
Demand of no man over-much.
Thou shalt not harbour bootless care,
Thou shalt not give, but freely share,
Thou shalt not meddle or condemn:
The souls of others leave to them.
No sap of life do thou destroy,
All things by faith thou shalt enjoy.
Weigh not on one thou holdest dear,
Above all else, thou shalt not fear.

SATURDAY—NOVEMBER 22.

WHEN I returned from work the other day and walked into our lounge, I couldn't, for a moment, make out what had happened. Then it dawned on me. The Lady of the House had been moving the furniture round!

" Don't look like that, Francis!" she said, as she came into the room, for I must have looked as though I didn't quite approve. " It's good to have a change now and again."

And so it is—in all sorts of things, even though we may resent it a bit at first. Remember, someone once said, " The only difference between a rut and a grave is its depth!"

SUNDAY—NOVEMBER 23.

LET your light so shine before men, that they may see your good works, and glorify your Father which is in heaven.   St Matthew 5, 16.

MONDAY—NOVEMBER 24.

THEY tell a story in Leeds of a traveller who, years ago, enquired the way to a neighbouring village. He was told, " Well, you can go by the top road or the bottom road."

" Which do you recommend?" asked the traveller.

" No, you must make up your own mind. Whichever way you go, you'll wish you'd taken the other! And when you get there, you'll probably wish you'd never gone!"

To laugh at pessimism like that can make optimists of us all!

TUESDAY—NOVEMBER 25.

I WONDER who now remembers Mairi Chisholm of Chisholm. She was the daughter of the chieftain of a Highland clan and as secretary of the Clan Association kept thousands in touch with the part of the world from which their ancestors had come.

But she deserves to be remembered for something even more important. She was one of the first women to ride a motor bike, and in 1914 she became a despatch rider for the Women's Emergency Corps. She drove an ambulance in Belgium right up to the front line of battle.

In the dark she often drove her heavy vehicle along rough tracks to pick up badly wounded men. At the first-aid post she would help to give emergency treatment, then drive the men to hospital 40 miles away. She was always in danger of shellfire and of gas attacks in which she herself suffered injury.

Perhaps all this seems a long time ago, but isn't it right that heroines like Mairi should still be remembered for their goodness and bravery?

HELLO?

Is that you, dear Granny? You've guessed this is me.
I'm ringing to ask if you're coming to tea.
I've set out a chair, put cakes on a plate,
So everything's ready—now, please don't be late!

WEDNESDAY—NOVEMBER 26.

IN one of his books, Dr Norman Vincent Peale, whose inspirational writings such as " The Power Of Positive Thinking " have brought help to many thousands of people, tells of a conversation he had with a prominent businessman during a plane flight.

The man clearly carried what to many would be an overwhelming burden of responsibility yet he obviously dealt with it all with a complete lack of tension and anxiety.

Dr Peale asked him what his secret was. " I simply begin and end each day calmly," was the reply.

" But how do you do that ?" persisted Dr Peale. The man went on to explain that he had committed to memory a number of inspirational passages which he repeated to himself morning and evening, meditating quietly on each. They included St Theresa's words, " Let nothing disturb you, let nothing frighten you. Everything passes away except God. God alone is sufficient."

From Robert Louis Stevenson he took, " Sit loosely in the saddle of life." And from the Bible, " In quietness and confidence shall be your strength."

Here indeed is a way to peace of mind and strength for living.

THURSDAY—NOVEMBER 27.

A YOUNG friend of ours, just before he left school, asked the various members of staff if they would write something in his autograph album.

His English master wrote this advice: " If you want to be happy and successful, be careful of your use of pronouns. Use ' you ' 20 times to every single use of ' I '."

THE FRIENDSHIP BOOK

I HAVE always admired Benjamin Franklin. Some time ago I was browsing through an old gardening book and was moved by the story of how, through exchanging letters on botany and gardens, a deep and affectionate friendship grew between Franklin, the great American statesman, and John Bartram, a simple Quaker farmer who had to work hard to read the letters and books that Franklin sent him about newly-discovered plants and trees. Franklin corresponded with Bartram for over 40 years.

The man of many parts and great achievements recognised and respected Bartram's homely wisdom and honest worth and was proud to call him friend.

ONCE there was a king who felt exceedingly unhappy because he thought there were no really good people left in his kingdom. So he said to a famous artist, " Paint me a picture of a really good person." The artist did so and the king was delighted. He stood back to admire the portrait and suddenly realised that all the features were familiar. He recognised the brow of his priest, the happy eyes of his minstrel, the lips of his small daughter, the lovely smile of his beloved wife, and so on.

The moral of the story being, of course, that there is no completely good person—but all the people round us have qualities to be admired.

WHOSOEVER shall compel thee to go a mile, go with him twain. St Matthew 5, 41.

DECEMBER

MONDAY—DECEMBER 1.

WHICH of us has not said at some time or other, " I'm at the end of my tether "? The other day I came across a saying which may help anyone who feels like that: " When you come to the end of your tether, tie a knot on it and hang on!"

TUESDAY—DECEMBER 2.

THE name Reginald Heber is familiar to many of us as the author of such hymns as " Holy, holy, holy, Lord God Almighty ", " From Greenland's icy mountains " and " The Son of God goes forth to war ".

After a brilliant academic career at Brasenose College, Oxford, Heber spent some time travelling abroad before being ordained in the Church of England. When he was only 40, he was appointed Bishop of Calcutta, a huge diocese which in those days included all India, Ceylon (now Sri Lanka) and Australia.

He quickly earned great regard for his pastoral care, his saintly character and his administrative ability, but he wore himself out with work and died at the age of 43.

His memorial is, deservedly, in St Paul's Cathedral and it describes him as being of " intense zeal and toleration ". What a remarkable tribute! There are many people who are zealous, but not very tolerant of other people and their views; often, too, there are tolerant people who seem to lack fire and zeal. Reginald Heber combined both qualities . . . a combination we might well try to emulate.

MY friend's teenage daughter left a note on the mantelpiece for her father to find when he came off nightshift: " Dear Dad, I am not working today—but please wake me anyway so I can enjoy going back to sleep again."

THURSDAY—DECEMBER 4.

A FAVOURITE hymn with many of us is Frances Ridley Havergal's,

Take my life and let it be
Consecrated Lord to Thee.

You may remember other verses of the hymn, too:
Take my voice and let me sing, Take my hands . . .
Take my feet. . . Take my intellect. . . Take my
will . . .

As a writer, pianist, singer and practising Christian we may be sure that these verses expressed Frances Havergal's own spirit of consecration. But one of the things that saddened her was that no opportunity seemed to open up to serve God on the mission field as she longed to do.

Then one day, she had an idea. She looked out a box which she hardly ever used. It contained a collection of jewellery — rings, bracelets, necklaces — many of them inherited. There and then she made a decision. She packed them up and sent them to the Church Missionary Society asking that they be sold and the proceeds devoted to the Society's work overseas. A simple act, but by doing it she felt she was now working in the mission field, too.

More than that, those other words of her hymn became marvellously true:

Take my silver and my gold,
Not a mite would I withold.

THE FRIENDSHIP BOOK

WHAT a problem it is sometimes buying Christmas presents, choosing the right gift for the right person, wondering whether it is really what they want.

The late Peter Marshall, one-time chaplain of the United States Senate, had something to say about this in a sermon entitled, " Let's Keep Christmas ":

" Perhaps there is nothing in the shop that they need. But what about some token of love— what about love itself . . . and friendship . . . and understanding . . . and consideration . . . and a helping hand . . . and a smile . . . and a prayer?

" You can't buy these in any shop, and these are the very things they need."

Well, we shall still want to buy our " hit-or-miss " gifts, but let's not forget the real gifts of Christmas.

A FRIEND of mine who is a college lecturer amused me recently when, in the course of conversation, the subject of " sleep learning " arose. This is the process by which people are supposed to be able to learn unconsciously by playing special cassettes under their pillow while they sleep.

" I don't believe a word of it, Francis," he retorted with a smile. " A lot of my students go to sleep during my lectures but they don't seem to learn very much in the process!"

LAY not up for yourselves treasures upon earth where moth and dust doth corrupt . . .

St Matthew 6, 19.

THE FRIENDSHIP BOOK

RECENTLY a woman remarked, " I never thought I'd join a pottery group, but I'm really keen now. Oh, I often make a mess of a vase or bowl, but it's all fun."

She has discovered the joy of doing something for its own sake and to widen her knowledge. Other people have found similar pleasure in improving their gardening knowledge or some other skill.

Years ago, someone wrote: " Whoever gets his soul into anything gets God into it."

That applies to newcomers trying out fresh hobbies, just as much as to great artists, musicians, actors and writers.

Sometimes we need to take a " journey into ourselves " to discover any buried talents or interests. And when discovered it is up to us to do something about them.

When he was 80, the writer Thomas Hardy remarked: " The older I grow, the less I find I know."

I TOOK a book round to Mr Jackson the other day. He is over 80 and he's been laid up with a backache caused, so his wife says, by splitting logs too vigorously.

" Perhaps this will help to pass the time," I said, as I handed over the book.

" Thank you," said Mr Jackson, " but I don't like the words ' pass the time '. Your book will help me to ' use the time '. At my age I am grateful for every minute of every day that is given to me."

There was a twinkle in his eye as he spoke, which softened the small rebuke. But I knew exactly what he meant. It's a mistake I won't make again.

THE FRIENDSHIP BOOK

MY thanks to Glenda Moore, of Dunscroft, near Doncaster, for this lovely poem:

> My grandmother's cottage,
>   I fondly recall,
> Had masses of roses
>   On its outside wall.
> While deep in the centre,
>   Beneath the old thatch,
> A warm welcome waited
>   The lift of the latch!
> Before the old fender,
>   The lamp light aglow,
> She'd tell of the splendour,
>   Of days long ago:
> Of candle-lit parlours,
>   High buttoned boots,
> Steam locomotives,
>   And dark Sunday suits;
> Brass warming-pans,
>   Her lace wedding gown,
> The old cherished hat
>   With the white satin crown.
> The cottage, and Grandma,
>   I remember them still,
> And her warm happy haven
>   At the foot of the hill.

AFTER a snowstorm that closed all the local schools, the teacher asked one small boy if he had used his time constructively while he had been off.

"Yes, Miss," he replied. "I prayed for more snow."

TENDER TRAP

Autumn berries, morning mist,
An artist's canvas hangs, dew-kissed;
Fragile, flimsy, spun with care,
A thing of beauty. Still, a snare.

N

FRIDAY—DECEMBER 12.

FIVE-YEAR-OLD Ellen had just visited Santa Claus in his grotto. " What did you ask him to bring you?" I asked, expecting the usual list of toys small children think up at such times. You can imagine my astonishment when the reply came: " Oh, I just told him to surprise me."

Israel was looking for a King, and God sent a new-born helpless baby. They expected the Messiah to come in power and wealth — he was born in a manger. What a surprise that was — and what an effect it had on the whole world!

SATURDAY—DECEMBER 13.

CHRISTMASTIME

WHAT does Christmas mean to us,
Does it mean a lot of fuss?
Gifts to buy and cards to write,
A Christmas tree with candles bright,
A turkey plump, mince pies to bake;
With outward signs we all partake.
We rush around, no time to pray,
" Oh, that can wait another day."
But stop awhile, just think it out
What Christmas Day is all about,
The day a tiny child was born,
In stable bare, and so forlorn,
The King of Kings who reigns above
Came down to bless us with his love.

SUNDAY—DECEMBER 14.

I HAD rather be a doorkeeper in the house of my God, than to dwell in the tents of wickedness.

Psalm 84, 10.

THE FRIENDSHIP BOOK

A BUSINESS friend has passed on to me a jingle that appears in a " hand-out " to salesmen in the firm for which he works:

" To sell John Brown what John Brown buys,
You've got to see things through John Brown's eyes."

Good advice—not just for salesmen but for all of us. To try to see things from the other person's point of view, to try to put ourselves in their position, is the surest way to real and lasting friendships.

K ISSING under the mistletoe seems to be entirely a British custom, and no-one seems quite sure how it originated.

Christina Hole, a folklore expert, suggests that it may be due to the fact that till at least the 17th century, kissing was a very common form of greeting in this country. Erasmus wrote " Wherever you go, everyone welcomes you with a kiss, the same on bidding farewell . . . kisses, kisses everywhere."

Mistletoe has long been regarded as the plant of peace. Traditionally, if enemies met under a tree on which mistletoe was growing they were expected to make up their quarrel there and then.

During the Middle Ages, there was a custom in York Minster of laying a branch of mistletoe on the high altar and leaving it there for the Twelve Days of Christmas. While it remained, a universal peace and pardon was proclaimed at the city gates.

No doubt we shall enjoy the traditional custom of kissing under the mistletoe, but don't let us forget the symbolism of mistletoe as the emblem of peace and love — the true marks of this Christmas season.

THE FRIENDSHIP BOOK

I LIKE the little story of the lady who wished to join a certain church but was worried about some new ideas they had introduced into the service.

" Is it true," she asked the minister, " that the Ten Commandments are repeated during the service?"

" Oh," he replied, " we have introduced a greater innovation than that."

" What is that?" she asked.

" We are trying to keep them."

EVERY Christmas for many years the Lady of the House and I have made a practice of re-reading Charles Dickens's " A Christmas Carol." Sometimes we read it to ourselves; other times we read passages aloud to each other.

Last Christmas I suggested that we should each choose our favourite passage from the story and read it aloud. And so we did—only to find that we had both chosen the same passage!

It was the one containing the words of Scrooge's nephew: " I have always thought of Christmastime as a good time; a kind, forgiving, charitable, pleasant time; the only time I know of, in the long calendar of the year, when men and women seem by one consent to open their shut up hearts freely. . . and therefore, though it has never put a scrap of gold or silver in my pocket, I believe that it *has* done me good, and *will* do me good: and I say, God bless it."

That seemed to us the heart of Dickens's Christmas story. It may not say *all* that ought to be said about Christmas, but would that everyone could capture at least that much of its spirit.

BURNING AMBITION

With pencil, paper, word and sum,
Preparing for the years to come.

THE FRIENDSHIP BOOK

A FRIEND tells me that he passed a church recently where there were two posters side by side. One read: " Preacher Next Sunday: Rev. John Smith."

The other, a Wayside Pulpit poster, said, " Don't worry. It may never happen."

JOHN and Emma were an elderly couple, who often had barely enough to make ends meet. One Christmas, Emma decided they would give themselves a treat: she would make a Christmas pudding.

However, when she saw the result—a huge, rich pudding—she felt it was an extravagance for the two of them, so she wrote an anonymous note, fastened it to the pudding, wrapped it up and placed it on the step of the local Children's Home.

Now, grateful as the Matron was, she really had more puddings than she knew what to do with, but she thought that the minister would appreciate it, so she left it on *his* doorstep.

But the minister was always thinking of others rather than himself. There must be someone in the village who needed this more than him—John and Emma, of course!

So the pudding completed its journey. Christmas is, after all, about giving—and receiving!

AND she shall bring forth a son, and thou shalt call his name Jesus: for he shall save his people from their sins.

St Matthew 1, 21.

THE FRIENDSHIP BOOK

MONDAY—DECEMBER 22.

GRANTLAND RICE was an American sportswriter who also wrote verses. This is one I remember:

For when the One Great Scorer comes to write against your name,
He marks—not that you won or lost—but how you played the game.

TUESDAY—DECEMBER 23.

A PSYCHOLOGIST who helped many hundreds of people to a new and hopeful attitude towards life said that two words occurred over and over again in the stories which his patients poured out to him. He called them " the two saddest words in the English language ". The words were, " If only . . ." — and they were used by people who were regretting something they had done in the past and wished that they had done something different.

He used to suggest that they should cut these words out of their vocabulary and learn, when faced with failure or disappointment, to say instead, " Next time . . ."

As we approach the end of this year and look forward to the beginning of another, let us fix our eyes, not on the failures of the past, but on the hopes and opportunities of the future.

WEDNESDAY—DECEMBER 24.

THE guest of honour at a Christmas dinner in the county town of Cornwall rose to speak.

He began: " You have been giving your attention to a turkey stuffed with sage. Will you now please give your attention to a sage stuffed with turkey . . !"

HERE'S God's Christmas Gift," said William Booth showing the new baby girl to his six other children on Christmas Day, 1865. Neither he, nor they, imagined that their new sister would become the first woman General of the Salvation Army.

As a schoolgirl, Evangeline Cory Booth, known as Eva to her family, took her first bundle of Salvationist magazines to sell in the East End of London. She learned of life among the poor and neglected; the suffering in the slum streets. Her apparent destitution while working as a flower girl caused an old man to advise, " Go to the Salvation Army. They'll help you," little knowing he was speaking to the founder's daughter.

When Eva became the head of the Army she firmly believed that any assistance to anyone down on their luck should be given in such a way that it did not injure their self-respect, but helped to restore a belief in a personal God who has the welfare of every human being at heart.

I HAVE quoted before from my old autograph album. Here is another verse which I have found helpful when confronted by some seemingly formidable task:

One step and then another,
And the longest walk is ended;
One stitch and then another,
And the largest rent is mended;
One brick upon another,
And the highest wall is made;
One flake upon another
And the deepest snow is laid.

AT SUNSET

When all the world is still, suspending time,
And space is beauty, gilded in the west,
Tarry a little, stand in wonder, friend.
Give thanks. A perfect day is laid to rest.

SATURDAY—DECEMBER 27.

THIS is a prayer specially written for Christmastime:

A prayer for you is said today:
May the love of God ever with you stay;
Wherever you are, whatever you do,
May the blessing of God ever rest on you;
And in the years that are still to come,
May the peace of God be in your home.
At Christmastide and in New Year, too,
May God's great love abide with you.

SUNDAY—DECEMBER 28.

WHEN they were come into the house, they saw the young child with Mary his mother, and fell down, and worshipped him.   St Matthew 2, 11.

MONDAY—DECEMBER 29.

AFTER her Sunday School class, my niece Joanna came to tea. She talked excitedly about the Nativity scene that she had helped to create out of a cardboard box, straw and other simple materials.

" We made shepherds out of dolls and sheep from pipe cleaners and cotton wool," Joanna enthused. " We also dressed three dolls in silky robes. They were the Wise Men who came a long way to give presents to the baby Jesus."

" And what did they give?" I asked, testing Joanna's memory.

" Gold, frankincense and mirth," she answered promptly. I liked that third gift. In all the rush and bustle of Christmas, I think it is important to remember that the basic message of Christmas is one of joy, gladness and goodwill.

THE FRIENDSHIP BOOK

JOHN RUSKIN, the 19th century author, was a great lover of the Lake District. He lived at Brantwood, Coniston. In his adult life he was often unhappy, but one spot always brought peace to his soul.

He loved the shores of Derwentwater, especially Friars Crag. On the Crag is his memorial, erected in 1900, with the quotation, " The first thing I remember as an event in life, was being taken by my nurse to the brow of Friars Crag, Derwentwater." These words and a medallion portrait of Ruskin are on one side. On the other is the form of a Celtic cross and an inscription:

" The Spirit of God is around you in the air you breathe. His glory is in the light you see, and in the fruitfulness of the earth and the joy of his creation. He has written for you day by day His revelation and He has granted you day by day your daily bread."

I LOVE the sound of bells—I think most of us do. I was reading recently an article about the making of bells, telling not only of the skill but also the love with which the craftsman does his work. The writer told of speaking to a bell-founder who had proudly shown him a bell he had just completed.

" Just look at her," he said. " She has a ' head ', a ' waist ', a ' mouth ', a ' lip '. She'll ' speak ' till her voice cracks with old age. It's hard to think of her not being alive!"

Fanciful, perhaps. Yet as we hear the bells welcoming in the New Year, bells which " ring out the old, ring in the new ", don't they speak to us a living message of joy and hope?

Where the Photographs were taken

AT REST — *Tarbert, Loch Fyne, Argyll.*

WINTER WALKERS — *Savernake Forest, Wiltshire.*

OYEZ! — *Dorchester, Dorset.*

NATURE'S BRUSH — *Woodham Walter, Essex.*

OLD WARRIOR — *HMS Victory, Portsmouth.*

CLOISTERS — *Worcester Cathedral.*

SEA MURMURS — *Near Newquay, Cornwall.*

IN THE WOODLAND — *Surrey.*

WISE FOREFATHERS — *Knaresborough, Yorkshire.*

QUIET WAYS — *Swan Green, Hampshire.*

MORNING BREAK — *Lynmouth, Devon.*

THEN AND NOW — *Winchester Cathedral.*

COOL WATERS — *Salisbury Cathedral and the River Avon, Wiltshire.*

GOLDEN DAYS — *Bournemouth.*

QUIET CORNER — *Mellerstain, Berwickshire.*

WELL DONE! — *Stirling Castle.*

YEAR ROUND — *Minterne Magna, Dorset.*

THE SENTINEL — *Ringstead Bay, Dorset.*

AT SUNSET — *Port Erin, Isle of Man.*

Printed and Published by D. C. THOMSON & CO. LTD.,
185 Fleet Street, London EC4A 2HS.

© D. C. Thomson & Co. Ltd., 1985.

ISBN 0 85116 345 9